S0-AMP-890

The Early Modern Englishwoman: A Facsimile Library of Essential Works

Series I

Printed Writings, 1500–1649: Part 3

Volume 1

Elizabeth Tyrwhit

The Early Modern Englishwoman: A Facsimile Library of Essential Works

Series I

Printed Writings, 1500–1640: Part 3

Volume 1

Elizabeth Tyrwhit

Selected and Introduced by
Patricia Brace

General Editors
Betty S. Travitsky and Anne Lake Prescott

ASHGATE

Published by
Ashgate Publishing Limited
Gower House
Croft Road
Aldershot
Hants GU11 3HR
England

Ashgate Publishing Company
Suite 420
101 Cherry Street
Burlington, VT 05401–4405
USA

Ashgate website: http://www.ashgate.com

British Library Cataloguing-in-Publication Data
Tyrwhit, Elizabeth
Elizabeth Tyrwhit. - (The early modern Englishwoman : a facsimile library of essential works. Printed writings 1500–1640, series 1 ; pt. 3, vol. 1)
1.Church of England - English 2.Prayer-books
I.Title II.Brace, Patricia
242.8'0342'09031

Library of Congress Cataloging-in-Publication Data
The early modern englishwoman: a facsimile library of essential works. Part 3. Printed writings, 1500–1640 / general editors, Betty S. Travitsky and Anne Lake Prescott.

See page vi for complete CIP Block 2002025877

The woodcut reproduced on the title page and on the case is from the title page of Margaret Roper's trans. of [Desiderius Erasmus] *A Devout Treatise upon the Pater Noster* (circa 1524).

ISBN 0 7546 0440 3

Printed in Great Britain by Antony Rowe Ltd, Chippenham, Wiltshire.

CONTENTS

Library of Congress Cataloging-in-Publication Data
Tyrwhit, Elizabeth.
[Morning and euening prayer]
Elizabeth Tyrwhit / [selected and introduced by] Patricia Brace.
p. cm. -- (The early modern Englishwoman. Printed writings, 1500-1640, Series 1, Part 3 ; v. 1)
Includes bibliographical references.
ISBN 0-7546-0440-3
1. Prayers--Early works to 1800. I. Brace, Patricia. II. Title. III. Series.

BV237 .T97 2002
242'.803--dc21

2002025877

PREFACE
BY THE GENERAL EDITORS

Until very recently, scholars of the early modern period have assumed that there were no Judith Shakespeares in early modern England. Much of the energy of the current generation of scholars has been devoted to constructing a history of early modern England that takes into account what women actually wrote, what women actually read, and what women actually did. In so doing the masculinist representation of early modern women, both in their own time and ours, is deconstructed. The study of early modern women has thus become one of the most important—indeed perhaps the most important—means for the rewriting of early modern history.

The Early Modern Englishwoman: A Facsimile Library of Essential Works is one of the developments of this energetic reappraisal of the period. As the names on our advisory board and our list of editors testify, it has been the beneficiary of scholarship in the field, and we hope it will also be an essential part of that scholarship's continuing momentum.

The Early Modern Englishwoman is designed to make available a comprehensive and focused collection of writings in English from 1500 to 1750, both by women and for and about them. The three series of *Printed Writings* (1500–1640, 1641–1700, and 1701–1750) provide a comprehensive if not entirely complete collection of the separately published writings by women. In reprinting these writings we intend to remedy one of the major obstacles to the advancement of feminist criticism of the early modern period, namely the limited availability of the very texts upon which the field is based. The volumes in the facsimile library reproduce carefully chosen copies of these texts, incorporating significant variants (usually in appendices). Each text is preceded by a short introduction providing an overview of the life and work of a writer along with a survey of important scholarship. These works, we strongly believe, deserve a large readership—of historians, literary critics, feminist critics, and non-specialist readers.

The Early Modern Englishwoman also includes separate facsimile series of *Essential Works for the Study of Early Modern Women* and of *Manuscript Writings*. These facsimile series are complemented by *The Early Modern Englishwoman 1500–1750: Contemporary Editions*. Also under our general editorship, this series will include both old-spelling and modernized editions of works by and about women and gender in early modern England.

New York City
2003

INTRODUCTORY NOTE

Elizabeth Tyrwhit's 1574 *Morning and Euening Praiers* (*STC* 24477.5) is a collection of private prayers, a class of books that grew in both popularity and volume with the establishment of Protestantism in England from the mid-century on. One of the most enduring was Katherine Parr's *Prayers or Medytacions*, which appeared in 13 editions from 1545 to 1640, and is bound with Tyrwhit's 1574 text. By contrast, Tyrwhit's appeared only once, although there was a later version in Bentley's 1582 *Monument of Matrones* (*STC* 1892).

Lady Elizabeth Tyrwhit

Tyrwhit was born at Brede, East Sussex, one of five children of Sir Goddard Oxenbridge and his second wife, Anne, daughter of Sir Thomas Fiennes (Cooper 58). She married Sir Robert Tyrwhit, who too served the royal household, between March 1538 and August 1539. While earlier accounts of Tyrwhit's life note that she married prior to 1546 (Cooper 62; Bell 199), a more precise date is determined through references to 'Mrs Oxenbridge' and 'Mrs Tyrwhit' in records around these two dates (Byrne 1125, 1126). Confusingly Tyrwhit's half-brother, Thomas, also had a daughter named Elizabeth who married a Robert Tyrwhit, niece and nephew, respectively, to the elder couple (Cooper 60).

The durability of Tyrwhit's career is one of the most fascinating features of her life, as she survived the turbulence of Henry VIII's court to serve four of his queens. She appears first in court records in 1537 as a recipient of gifts and as a Gentlewoman of the Privy Chamber to Jane Seymour (Henry VIII 12:973i; 15:21; 16:1389). She appears as a signatory, along with others of the Ladies of the Queen's Privy Chamber, to a letter to Henry, in August 1539, admiring his new battleship (Byrne 1513a). Her relationship with Katherine

Parr was especially close, possibly because Parr was cousin by marriage to Robert Tyrwhit through her own marriage to Edward, Lord Borough (Tyrwhitt 25). Certainly, Tyrwhit shared Parr's Protestant sympathies. In 1546, when Henry suspected links between Katherine Parr's household and the Protestant martyr, Anne Askew, Tyrwhit was one of three Reformist ladies identified for arrest and interrogation; the others were Lady Anne Herbert and Lady Lane (Weir 1991 517–23). In recognition of her ardently Reformist leanings, Tyrwhit's husband noted that 'my wyffe is not sayne in Dyvinity, but is half a Scripture woman' (Haynes 104). By her own account Tyrwhit attended Parr at Sudeley Castle during both the birth of Parr's daughter and her subsequent death from puerperal fever (Haynes 104).

However, she entered most fully into court drama when, in 1547–48, Princess Elizabeth lived with Katherine Parr and her fourth husband, Thomas Seymour, Lord High Admiral and brother of Protector Somerset. During this time Seymour appears to have developed a pronounced sexual interest in the princess, a dalliance to which Parr put a stop in the summer of 1548 by removing her to the household of Lord Denny. After Parr's death, however, Seymour's interest in Elizabeth re-emerged and culminated in, at the very least, some fishing for information from her cofferer, Thomas Parry, and governess, Katherine Ashley. At most, these two figures conspired with Seymour to plot a secret marriage, unapproved by Edward. This episode became a lever in a power struggle between Seymour and Somerset (Haynes 105, 107) because such plans for an illicit marriage became grounds for a charge of treason and Seymour's subsequent execution. Investigation of Seymour's actions was carried out by Robert Tyrwhit, Elizabeth Tyrwhit's husband and an agent of the Council, who served in a number of other capacities in the households of both Henry VIII and Edward VI. At the instigation of the Council, after Robert Tyrwhit's interrogation failed to uncover evidence of participation by Princess Elizabeth (Haynes 102), a false 'friend' was planted in the household in an effort to win her confidence, and Elizabeth Tyrwhit took over Katherine Ashley's position (Haynes 107). After this point Tyrwhit disappears from the records of royal households, although she was the dedicatee of John Field's 1577 translation of Jean de l'Espine's *Treatise on Christian Righteousness* (3–6). According to her will, proved April 23rd (P.C.C. PROB11/60 18 Langley), Tyrwhit died in 1578 in Clerkenwell, predeceased by both her husband, Robert (1572), and their only child, a daughter named Katherine (1567).

Morning and Euening Praiers

Of considerable interest is the tiny gilt girdle-book in which Tyrwhit's text first appeared, in part because a handwritten note on a now lost blank page apparently indicated that the girdle-book belonged to Elizabeth I (Nichols xxxvii). Along with Tyrwhit's work it contains the Litany, an incomplete copy of *The Queenes Prayers* by Katherine Parr, and an imperfect copy of a 'Kalender'. The text appears to have been cut down to fit the binding, and some gatherings of Parr's work to have been removed for this purpose. The book's opulent, enamelled gold binding depicts Moses raising the serpent and the judgment of Solomon on front and back covers respectively. The former is surrounded by the phrase, 'Make the afyrye [i.e., thee afiery] serpent an [sic] settt [sic] vp for a sygne that as many as are bytte maye loke vpon it an [sic] lyve', while the border around the latter says, 'Then the kyng ansvered an [sic] sayd gyve her the lyvyng child an slaye t [sic] not for she is the mother thereof'. The binding, which dates from about 1540, is the work of the Flemish goldsmith Hans von Antwerpen, who had received several royal commissions by this time (Tait 1985 39; 1991 113–14). The Oxenbridge family arms appear on the verso of the title page.

Morning and Euening Praiers was published with the Litany in a single edition in 1574 by Christopher Barker (who also published Anne Cooke Bacon's translations of Bernardino Ochino) with a heavily altered version appearing in the 'Second Lampe of Virginitie' of *The Monument of Matrones*. As an example of a 'tablett', or girdle-prayerbook, the book exemplifies a fashion of the second quarter of the sixteenth century (Tait 1985 30), a period that corresponds with the political and religious upheaval of the continuing English Reformation. As such it joins the spiritual with the political, the domestic with the public, for it is both an intimate piece of jewelry and an example of explicitly Protestant theology, simultaneously the subject of public debate and legislation. In relation to the other texts in the volume, Tyrwhit's participates in a similar amalgamation, for *The Queenes Prayers* emphasize the relationship between the individual soul and God, while the Litany is part of public liturgy. Tyrwhit combines the two emphases by creating a collection of highly individual prayers, psalms, meditations and hymns that adapt the Anglican liturgies for morning and evening prayer.

In her preface, 'A briefe exhortation vnto prayer', Tyrwhit exploits this dual focus to produce a powerful narrative. The tone of the prefatory 'exhortation' is, as its title suggests, imperative, a mood reflected in its opening phrases: 'Let not to praye'; 'stand not in feare'; and 'prepare thy soule'. Here, speaker stands in relation to audience as priest to congregation by instructing it in its task. In the next section, Tyrwhit shifts the imperative to the first-person plural, including herself with phrases like 'We must consider therefore when wee pray, in whose presence we stand' and 'wee must therefore diligently and wyth all reuerence and godly feare, endeuer oure selues to remoue all such thinges as maye offende his diuine maiesty'. She performs another priestly function here by rhetorically calling the congregation together around her. The remainder of the preface emphasizes the same kind of calling together, but in a divine, rather than human, context 'whereby our mindes are caried [sic] hither & thither, and beinge drawne out of Heauen, and frō the pure beholding of God are pressed down vnto the earth'. The language is of progress beyond self, in which the heart is 'lifted vp aboue itself' and 'mouth, spirit & hart be eleuated mindfully in faith'. Finally, she identifies this movement toward God as the 'chief dutie of prayer'. Both speaker and book are granted considerable agency, as the former draws the community together, while the latter provides the prayers that help to draw the individual beyond the bounds of self into communion with God.

The structure of the text extends Tyrwhit's prefatory discussion. While the prayers, psalms, anthems and hymns emphasize the personal, volitional nature of devotion by speaking in the first person, the rubrics and broader structures of the volume sustain the guiding/

teaching mode established by the imperative mood of the preface. Unlike other collections of private devotions (for example Parr's *Prayers or Medytacions* in the same volume) in which the sequence of prayers is determined internally and traces an individual, spiritual narrative, Tyrwhit's work is organized, to a significant extent, externally and liturgically. The devotional material is divided into offices for morning and evening that follow roughly the orders of service found in the Book of Common Prayer in terms of both content and sequence. The generic clustering of 'Certaine Godly Sentences' with other prayers and hymns after the offices also mimics the Prayer Book's grouping of collects and prayers specific to particular moments in the liturgical calendar.

Despite her being 'half a Scripture woman', the presence of phrases drawn from daily offices throughout her collection indicates Tyrwhit's liturgical orientation. Indeed, the opening confession echoes the phrasing of the general confessions used for Morning Prayer and Holy Communion, but in the first person singular. Later, the versicles and responses from the Book of Common Prayer's morning and evening services appear, again adapted to suit the individual speaker. The benediction on C6v–C7r, based on Numbers 6:24–26, echoes closely a frequently used blessing. In Tyrwhit's evening prayers, the psalm and prayer at D2r–D3v roughly paraphrase the Magnificat and Nunc Dimittis, while her prayer at F1r–v revises the intercessory Prayer for the Sick.

Simultaneously, however, reformist concern for self-examination and meditation is readily apparent in the psalms, meditations and hymns. The three psalms in the office of morning prayer reflect Tyrwhit's broader strategy of appropriation and adaptation. None appears to be taken from either a current translation of the Bible or from an edition of the Book of Common Prayer. Rather they appear to be loose paraphrases of Psalms 5 (B4r), 1 (B6r) and 25 (B8r), with emphasis on the potential for individual spiritual growth and development and on God's mercy, rather than on His judgment. For example Psalm 1 focusses on the central organic image of the soul as a tree nourished by God's spirit, while Psalm 25 presents the relationship between the speaker and God as an exchange in which attention to or searching for God is rewarded with revelation and mercy. In the latter, the imperative mood of the prefatory 'exhortation' remains. In keeping with the broad rhetorical strategy of the work, the 'Certain Godly Sentences' that follow the offices contain aphoristic wisdom not unlike Proverbs. These statements thus extend the purview of the book beyond the ritual of offering private prayers to advice for living the life of the spirit in the world.

The final group of prayers and meditations again takes liturgy as its point of departure but expands first spatially, moving from the self to a broader social world, then temporally, from the present to eternal life. The first of these two subgroups draws on the Anglican liturgical tradition of intercessory prayers that call attention to the concerns of the community. Accordingly, Tyrwhit begins with a prayer for individual protection from the dangers of the world, expanding to friends and then to the health and wisdom of the Queen, all petitions concerned with the well-being of the secular state. These prayers are followed by prayers for the sick or those in sorrow and adversity, especially those who risk their lives for the proclamation of the Gospel, and for the stopping of the mouths of adversaries who threaten the domain of the spirit. In the final set of meditations, Tyrwhit moves from the divine to the human and back again, first through a prayer to the Trinity, which is followed by a contemplation of the human Christ's passion paired with a meditation on human misery. The final pair of prayers completes the return to the divine domain by repeating explicitly the pattern of the Fall and human death (implied in the opening prayer on the Trinity) and concluding with a meditation on judgment and eternal life.

These carefully structured prayers and meditations are followed by a series of hymns, in fourteeners, which caused W.D. Cooper to note that if Lady Elizabeth was 'one of the earliest and one of the most pious, she was also one of the most prosaic of our Sussex poets' (63) and Elaine Beilin to comment that 'if her prayers lack the poetic skill to move the reader deeply, they still accomplish their probable intention to bear witness to Lady Tyrwhitt's faith' (81). These hymns are certainly less inspired than the earlier sections of the work.

While Tyrwhit's text was not republished except in a nineteenth-century edition of Bentley, the book in which it was bound has an interesting history as a bibliographical artifact. In 1788 it came into the possession of George Ashby, who could trace its ownership through his wife's family back to the early seventeenth century, and became the focus of lengthy bibliophilic discussion in *The Gentleman's Magazine* from 1789 to 1791, spurred by the similarity of its binding to a silver one of Parr's *Prayers or Medytacions*. It is also mentioned twice in the nineteenth century. The first instance, in an auction catalogue, terms it one of the 'interesting historical curiosities' from the Duke of Sussex's library:

> QUEEN ELIZABETH'S PRAYER BOOK, printed by Barker, in a case of gold, beautifully chased with sacred subjects, and partly enamelled; this highly interesting relic was presented by Lady G. Tirwitt [sic] to Queen Elizabeth, when a prisoner in the Tower, and was generally worn by the Queen suspended from a gold chain. (*Catalogue* 51)

This citation reinscribes the popular legend about the relationship between the book and Elizabeth I, both elements of which may be true independently, although not together. The binding, with other contents, may have been a gift to the young Elizabeth at that time, and the book after its publication in 1574, but they could not have been given together. Later, an engraving of the binding appeared in *The Illustrated London News* (6 April, 1850) as part of an account of an exhibit of privately-owned treasures. The book then passed through several hands until 1894 when Sir Augustus Wollaston Franks gave it to The British Museum, where the 32° volume now resides in a case of Tudor jewelry.

When Tyrwhit's work reappears in Thomas Bentley's *Monument of Matrones*, the editor's hand is palpable. He has organized the contents of the anthology into 'Lamps of Virginitie', understood to represent 'these seuen Lamps of your [Elizabeth I's] perpetuall virginitie, to remaine vnto women as one entire and goodlie monument of praier, precepts, and examples meet for meditation, instruction, and imitation to all posteritie' (B1r). The task of these writers, according to Bentley's preface, is 'to shew themselues woorthie paternes of all pietie, godlinesse and religion to their sex, and for the common benefit of their countrie, … to spend their time, their wits, their substance… in compiling and translating of sundrie most christian and godlie bookes…' (B1r). In the process of locating Tyrwhit in the 'Second Lampe of Virginitie', Bentley removes her preface and restructures the text so that the intercessory prayers, meditations and hymns appear integrated into the orders of service with the 'Certain Godly Sentences' appended. This reshaping is significant because it reframes Tyrwhit's text as part of a corpus of texts by Protestant female worthies, rather than as a priestly guide. Tyrwhit's agency in the shaping of the individual spiritual journey is absorbed completely into official liturgical structures, just as Tyrwhit's book itself becomes an appendage to the chaste body of her queen.

We reprint below the unique British Museum copy of Tyrwhit's original volume, since alterations in Bentley's edition were likely made after Tyrwhit's death and thus without her participation.

Acknowledgements

Thanks to Dr. Dora Thornton, Keeper of Medieval and Later Antiquities, British Museum, for her generous assistance and to the Advisory Research Council, Queen's University, Kingston, for the research funds for this project.

References

STC 24477.5 [Tyrwhit]

STC 4 826.6 [Parr]

(1843), *Catalogue of the truly magnificent Collection of ancient and modern … Plate (of…Portraits in Oils, etc.-of… Rings, Seals, etc.-of Regulators, Clocks, etc.-of…Furniture, etc.-of Pipes, etc.) of … the Duke of Sussex … which will be sold by auction, etc*, London: Christie and Manson

(1850), *The Illustrated London News*, 6th April

Beilin, Elaine (1987), *Redeeming Eve*, Princeton: Princeton University Press

Bell, Maureen, George Parfitt and Simon Shepherd (1990), *A Biographical Dictionary of English Women Writers, 1580–1720*, New York: Harvester, p. 199

Byrne, Muriel St. Clare (ed.) (1981), *The L'Isle Letters*, Vol. 5, Chicago: University of Chicago Press

Cooper, William Durrant (1856), *Contributions to the Eighth Volume of the Sussex Archeological Collections, containing notices of the last of the Braose Family; the Family of Lord Hoo and Hastings; The Town of Winchelsea in and after the Fifteenth Century; and of the Family of Oxenbridge, of Forde Place, Brede, and Winchelsea*, London: John Russell Smith, pp. 52–63

Field, John, trans. (1577), *An Excellent Treatise of Christian Righteousness, written first in the French tongue by M.I. de l'Espine...*, London: T. Vautrolier

Great Britain, Record Commission (1856–72), *Calendar of state papers. Domestic series of the reign of Edward VI, Mary and Elizabeth 1547–80*, Robert Lemon (ed.) and M.A.E. Green. London: H.M.S.O.

Great Britain, Record Commission (1830–52), *Calendar of state papers. Domestic series of the reign of Henry the eighth, 1518–1547, preserved in the Public Record Office*, London: H.M.S.O.

Haynes, Samuel (1740), *A Collection of State Papers Relating to Affairs in the Reigns of King Henry VIII, King Edward VI, Queen Mary and Queen Elizabeth, from the year 1542 to 1570... Left by William Cecill Lord Burghley and Now remaining at Hatfield House, in the Library of the Right Honourable the present Earl of Salisbury*, London: William Bowyer

Nichols, John (1823), *The Progresses and Public Processions of Queen Elizabeth...Collected from original manuscripts, scarce pamphlets, corporation records, parochial registers, &c, &c. A new edition in three volumes*, London: John Nichols and Son

Partnow, E. (ed.) (1986), *The Quotable Woman: From Eve to 1799*, New York: Facts on File

Strickland, Agnes (1864), *Lives of the Queens of England*, Vol. 3, London: Bell and Daldy

Tait, Hugh (1985), 'The girdle-prayerbook or "tablett": an important class of Renaissance jewellery at the court of Henry VIII', *Jewellery Studies*, Vol. 2, pp. 29–57

— (1991), "Goldsmiths and their Work at the Court of Henry VIII." *Henry VIII: A European Court in England*, London: Collins and Brown, pp. 112–17

— (1962), "Historiated Tudor Jewellery", *Antiquaries Journal*, XLII, part II, pp. 226–46

Tyrwhit, Elizabeth (1578) 'Will', P.R.O. P.C.C. PROB 11/60 18 Langley

Urban, Sylvanus (1790), *The Gentleman's Magazine and Historical Chronicle*, Volume XL, Part the Second, London: John Nichols for David Henry, pp. 703–988

— (1791), *The Gentleman's Magazine and Historical Chronicle*, Volume XLI, Part the First, London: John Nichols for David Henry, pp. 28–9

Weir, Alison (1996), *Children of England: The Heirs of King Henry VIII 1547–1558*, London: Pimlico, pp. 65–80

— (1991), *The Six Wives of Henry VIII*, London: The Bodley Head, pp. 517–59

PATRICIA BRACE

Morning and Euening Praiers (*STC* 24477.5; BL shelfmark Mic.A.17425) is reproduced, by permission, from the copy at the Department of Medieval and Later Antiquities, The British Museum. The text block measures 34 × 45 mm.

Words that are blotted or illegible in the original

B4v.5 comforte
D2r.4 magnified
  12 firmament
F1v.1 offences
  8 malice
F2r.9 stoppe
  10–11 ungodly
  11–12 gospell
  12 winne
G1v.12 prayed
H2r. 10 sittes
  12 tongs
  15 from
M1r.1 may euermore give
  13 old

Sigs. H7v and H8r are reversed in the original.

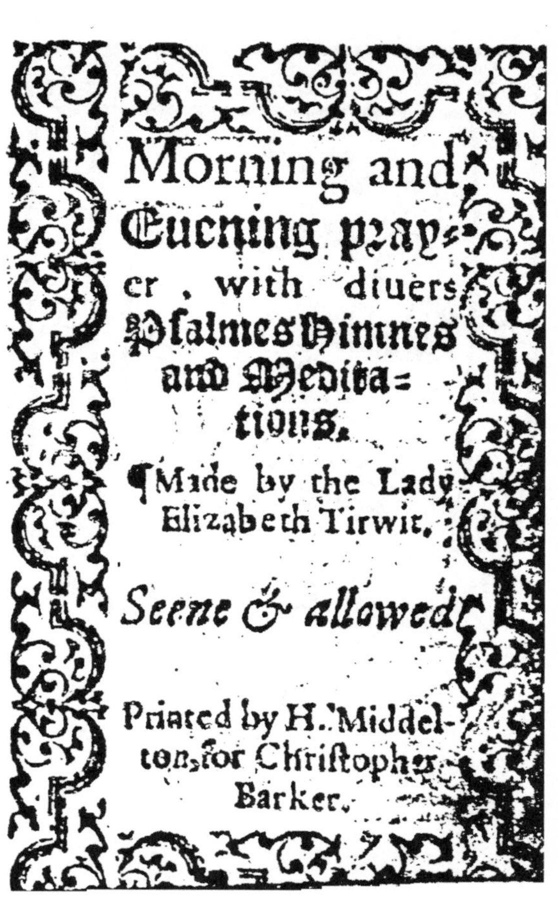

Morning and
Euening pray-
er, with diuers
Psalmes Himnes
and Medita-
tions.

¶Made by the Lady
Elizabeth Tirwit.

Seene & allowed.

Printed by H. Middel-
ton, for Christopher
Barker.

A briefe exhortation vnto Prayer.

Et not to praye alway, and ſtand not in feare to be refourmed vnto death, for the rewarde of God endureth for euer.

 Be

Before thou prayeſt prepare thy ſoule, & bee not as one that tempteth God.

VVee muſt conſider therefore when wee pray, in whoſe preſence we ſtand, to whom we ſpeake, & what we deſire. VVe

ſtand

ſtand in the preſencē of the Almightye Creator of Heauen and Earth, and all thinges therein conteyned, to whoſe eternall maieſtie innumerable thouſādſ of Angels do aſsiſt, ſerue & obey. VVe ſpeak vnto him who knoweth the ſecrets of our hartes, before whome nothing is more odious than hypocriſie and diſsimulation. VVe aſke thoſe things that are moſt to his glory, & the comfort of our

con-

conſcience. VVee muſt therefore diligently and wyth all reuerence and godly feare, endeuer oure ſelues to remoue all ſuch thinges as maye offende his diuine maieſty, to the vtter moſt of our power:

and first that we bee free from all worldly cares and fleshly cogitations, whereby our mindes are caried hither & thither, and beinge drawne out of Heauen, and frō the pure beholding of God are pressed

ſed downe vnto the earth. VVee muſt haue our harte not onely bent to praier, but as muche as is poſsible lifted vp aboue it ſelf, euen vnto that puritie which is worthy for God. VVe muſt alſo haue regarde that oure mouth, ſpirit & hart be eleuated mindfully in faith, for God is a ſpirite, and will be worshipt in ſpirit and truth, that is, in the godly affections of the hart, and with a trew, faithfull, and

vn-

vnfained woorship: and therfore as at all other times he requireth the hart, so specially when we shew our selues in his presence, and enter into cõmunication with him, and thereuppõ whẽ he promiseth to

heare

heare all those that call vppon him, hee maketh a restraint and saith that do call vppon him in truth. Seeing therefore the chiefe dutie of prayer consisteth in the hart, wee must with our whole hart pour out our prayers vnto God the ſearcher of harts, & with a ſincére, vnfayned & ardent affectiō & opening of our harts before God, call on him, els we shall not find him, but if wee call vppon him with

a

a ſure faith wee shall be ſure that hee will heare our petitions. Therefore vnto him be all honour, glory and praiſe for euer and euer. So be it.

A confeſsion to be ſayde before the morning prayer.

I Doe acknowledge and cõfeſſe vnto thee O moſt mercifull and Heauenly father, mine often and greuous offences that I haue committed againſt thy dyuine maieſtie, fro my youth hitherto, in thought, word and deede, leauing vndon e thoſe things which I oght and ſhould haue done, and doing thoſe thinges which

I

A Confession.

I ought not to haue done, prouoking thy wrath and indignation against mee, & nowe lamenting this my wickednesse, I appeal vnto thy mercy, and say with the Publican, O lord God be merciful vnto me a most wretched sinner, forgiue al that is paste, saue and defend me fro euill, and confirme me in good life, to the glory of thy name. So be it.

A

A prayer to bee saide at the vprising.

I Do thanke thee my most mercifull and heauenly father, by thy dearely beloued sonne Jesu Christ, that this night thou haste giuen mee sleepe and reste, preseruing mee from hurt and perill, I crie thee mercy for my offences, and I doe most humbly beeseeche thee, that thou wilt likewise this day keepe me frō sinne and all euill, so that

At the vprising.

all my thoughtes, wordes, and workes maye please thee: I do commit my self, both body and soule, and al thinges that I go aboute, into thy handes, beseeching thee that thi holy spirit mai abide with mee, leaste my deadly aduersary the Diuell haue power ouer me.

An Antheme.

HIS dearelye beloued son God did not spare, but for vs all deliuered him, how shall he not with him

him giue vs althings also.

A prayer to God the Father.

OUr mercifull Father which in teachinge vs to pray, by thy Sonne Christ haste commaunded vs to call thee father, & too beleeue that wee are thy beloued children, who stirrest vp none of thine too pray but to ye intent yt thou wouldest heare them, giuing vnto vs also al things more effectuously and plen teously, than we can either aske or thinke. We doe beseech thee for thy Sonnes sake, to geue vs grace too beleeue, and know assuredly that thy sonne our Sauiour Christ is geuen of thee vnto vs to be our Sauiour, our righteousnesse, our wisedome, our holynesse, our redemption, and our satisfaction. O Lorde suffer vs not to trust in any other saluation, but in thy sonne, and by thy sonne our sauiour Jesus Christ, So be it.

Morning prayer.

Our Father, &c.

Lorde open thou my lips, & my mouth may speake & shewe foorth that which is to thy glory and prayse: and shut my mouth from speaking of any thing whereby I shuld offend thy diuine maiestie.

or be hurtfull to my neighbour.

O God make ſpeede to ſaue vs.

O Lorde make haſte to helpe vs.

Glory be to the Father, to the Sonne, and to the holy Ghoſt.

As it was in the beginning, is now and euer ſhall be, world without end. Amen.

Praise ye the Lord.
Thankes be given unto God.

The first Psalme at morning prayer.

O Lord hear my words, marke my crying, O my king and my God, for unto thee only come I to pray: neither do I looke for succour any where els than of thee.

O Lord I beseech thee,

that thou wilt graciously hearken to my petitions, that thy grace may springe in my hart with the morow lighte of thy cōforte, the night of care and perturbatiō being ouerpassed: suffer me not to perishe with the vngodly folke, whom thou cursest.

I come running to thee, not trusting in mine owne righteousnesse, but to thy great and manifolde mercies.

O Lorde with the rule of thy iustice will I bee directed, for thy names sake, make plaine thy waye before me, and my way before thee, least the spirite of malice do turne mee thence.

Let them reioice that repose themselues, and trust alwaies in thy mercy, let them singe Hymnes and Psalmes, which do glory and reioyce in thee, let the triumphe which loue thy name.

Defend mee O Lorde, with thy grace as with a shield in time of perill, to theintent that when I am assaulted with them, I maye yet wyth constant cheere, growe vp vnto my full perfection.

Glory bee to the Father and to the sonne. &c.

As it was in the beginning, is now. &c.

A prayer.

prayer.

OH Lord God and Father, I beeseech thee by christ our lord, that of thy infinite mercy thou keepe me, so as at no time I follow the councell of the ungodly which knowe thee not, or of hipocrites, which with their hartes seke thee not.

A Psalme.

O Lord, suffer me not to enter into the way of sinners with a minde

to

to fulfil the desires & lustes of the flesh.

But whensoeuer thorough frailtie of my corrupt nature I shal chance to runne astray, then O Lord stay mee and plucke my foote backe againe.

Keepe me, that I sit not in the seate of pestilent scorners, which cloking their Pharisaicall and diuelish intents, condemne in other men thy veritie and Gospell.

prayer.

O Lorde bring to paſſe that I maye burne in the deſire of thy law, that vpon the aduauncement of thy word, my minde maye alwayes be occupied, that I may euermore chooſe that which is moſt pleaſaunt to thee, and hate that both in my ſelfe and others, which to thee is diſpleaſant.

Make I pray thee, that I may bee a tree planted by the ſweete Riuers of thy ghoſtly waters, to the

in-

intent I may bring forth fruite to thy glory and to the profit of my neighbour as often as thou shalt minister time & occasion therunto.

Least my leaues, which is my words & works, shall fade and fal away, but that all thinges maye prosper, whatsoeuer I shall doe in thy name: assist mee I beseech thee.

And graunt O most mercifull Father, that for Je-

su

in Christes sake, I maye
take roote in the ground of
lyfe, least with the vngod=
ly like chaffe and duste I
bee blowne abroade with
the most pernicious windes
of this world, and graunt
that I may stand in the as=
sembly of the righteous, &
yͭ I may enter into iudge=
ment by thy mercy with=
out punishment, and that
I may escape euerlastinge
damnation.

Glo

Glory be to the. &c.
As it was in the. &c.

An other Psalme.

TO thee O Lord I lift up my mind, in thee I trust O Lord God, let me not be confounded, least my enemies make me a iesting stocke, and a matter to laugh at.

O Lord make thy wayes knowne unto mee, & trade me in thy pathes.

Direct

prayer.

Direct me in thy trueth, and instruct mee, for thou art God my Sauiour, I looke after thee euery day.

O Lord thou art sweete and rightfull, and bringest againe into the way them which went out.

Thou leadest strait into thy iudgement thē, that bee milde and tractable, & teachest them that be meek thy word and testimonies.

Thou healest them that be contrite in hart, and asswagest their paines and grief.

Thou holdest vp all thē which els should fall, and all that are falne thou liftest vp againe.

Thou giuest sight to the blind, and losest them that be bound.

Thou art nie vnto all them that call vppon thee, so that they call vppon thee faithfully and hartely.

Thou fulfillest the desire of them that do feare thee,

and hearest their prayer, & sauest them.

Haue mercy vppon mee (O God) haue mercy vp=pon me, for in thee my soule trusteth.

Verely my soule hath a speciall respect to thee: for my health, my glory, and al my strength commeth fro thee.

For thy owne sake (O Lorde God) laye not my sinnes to my charge.

I vnderstand not all

mine errours: innumerable troubles doe close mee round about, my sinnes haue taken hold vpon me, and I am not able to looke vp.

Put to thy hand to help me, and lead me right in al my workes.

Make me to walke perfectly in thy waies, that no kind of sinne ouercome me.

Set a watch before my mouth, & keepe the doore of my lippes.

Let

Let the wordes of my mouth, and the meditation of my heart, be euer pleasaunt and acceptable in thy sight.

Let the woord of truth neuer goe away from my mouth, and suffer no malice to dwell in my hart.

O Lord deliuer my soule from lying lips, and saue me from a deceiptful tong.

Put into my mouth thy true and holy woord, and take from me all idle and vnfruitfull speech.

Deliuer mee from false surmises and accusations of men, rule mee euen as thou thinkest good, after thy will and pleasure.

Turne away mine eyes, that they behold no vaine thinges, fasten them in thy way.

Take from me fornication and all vncleannesse & let not the loue of the flesh beguile me.

Yea deliuer my soule frō pride,

pride, that it do not raigne in me, and then I shall bee cleane from the greatest sinne.

Stay and kepe my feete from euery euill way, least my steppes swarue from thy pathes.

My eyes looke euer vnto thee O Lord, bycause thou art nie at hand, and al thy wayes be truth.

Thy mercies bee great and many (O Lord) blessed is hee who so euer trussteth in thee.

For when I sayd vnto thee, my feete bee slipped, thy mercy O Lord by and by did hold me vp.

Teach me to do thy wil, and lead mee by thy path way, for thou art my God.

Oh lord, saue my soule, and deliuer mee from the power of darknesse.

Let the brightnesse of thy face shine vpon thy seruāt, for vnto thee O lord God, I haue fled for succour.

Looke

Looke vnto me and haue mercy vpon me, for I am deſolate and poore.

Keepe my ſoule, and deliuer me that I be not confoũded; for I haue truſted in thee.

O Lord God forſake me not, although I haue done no good in thy ſight.

For thy goodneſſe graũt mee, that at the leaſt wiſe now I maye begin to liue well. Amen.

O Lord ſhew thy ſeruants

uants thy workes, & their children thy glory, and the gracious Maiestie of the Lord our god be vpon vs. Oh prosper thou ỹ works of our handes, oh prosper thou our handie worke.

Glory be to the father. &c

As it was in the. &c.

Let vs pray.

O GOD that art the strength of such as trust in thee, merciful=ly

prayer.

ly assist vs that call vp pon thy name, and for as much as mans infirmitie can doe nothinge without thee, graunt I most humbly be seech thee, the helpe of thy spirite, that fulfilling thy commaundements both in will & deede, I may please thee through Jesus christ our Lord. So be it.

OH Lord blesse mee and defend me, O Lord lift vp thy countenaunce

ouer

ouer me, and bee mercifull vnto me: O Lord lift vp thy countenance ouer mee and giue me thy peace, that in thy peace, O Lord, I may depart, to amend my life, and do vnto the poore as much as I can, giue me grace to bee at vnitie, in quietnesse, and in charitie with all thy chosen and elect people, and that thy feare O Lord, may rest in my heart. So be it.

Prayse bee vnto God,

peace to the liuing, as they that depart in thy faith do rest in thee.

An other morning prayer by VV.B.

O Blessed Jesu, this day I commend me and all my proceedinges into thy hāds, this day I most humbly pray thee to helpe me, which hast made mee to thine owne Image, and in thy bloud hast clensed me,

me, which art my hope in
heauineſſe, my comfort in
care, and truſt in trouble,
although ſweete Lord, my
conſcience accuſeth me, and
the lawe condemneth mee,
yet thy precious death and
Teſtament hath deliuered
me with thee to raigne in
glory, after death hath a=
reſted me and the earth cō=
ſumed me: yet good Lord
I truſt in the reſurrection
to dwell with thee eternal
ly, thorowe they promiſe
made

made to me and to all that doe beleue in thee, and call vpon thy holy name: Thy kingdome come this daye to me, from Sathan deliuer me, with the bread of Angels feede mee, from fleshly lustes purge mee, from sodaine death & deadly sinne, O Lord take me. Giue me an hart to beleue in thee, and that all my senses may obey thee: and of thy mercy accept my prayer: this daye before thee,

which

Which art one GOD in Trinitie, to whom be honour and glo=rie. Amen.

(.·.)

Our father. &c.

And lead vs not into. &c.

But deliuer vs from euill. Amen.

Euening praier

COnuert vs our Sauiour & turne away thy wrath frõ vs.

O God make speede to saue vs:

O Lord make hast to helpe vs.

Glory be to the Father, to the sonne, and to the holy ghost.

Euening

As it was in the begin-
ning is now, and euer shal
be, world without end. A-
men.
Prayse ye the Lord.
Thankes be giuen
vnto God.

A Psalme.

BLessed art thou, O lord
God of our Fathers,
for thou art prayse and honour woorthy, and to bee
magnified for euer.

Bles-

Blessed bee the glory of thy holy name, for it is worthy to be praysed, and aboue all to bee magnified for euer.

Blessed art thou, O father, sonne, and holy ghost for thou art worthy to bee praysed, and aboue all to be magnified for euer.

Blessed bee thou in the firmament of heauen, for thou art prayse worthy for euer.

O geue thankes vnto the

Lord all his creatures, for he is kind harted and mercifull: yea his mercy endureth for euer.

Oh prayse him and geue him thankes, for his mercie endureth for euer, and world without end. Amen

A prayer.

Thy clemencie and blessing, O most mightie God, we doe craue and require of thee full instantly,

ly, let thy coũtenance shine on vs, haue compassion vpon vs, that here in earth we may find out the waye which leadeth vnto thee, and make vs to attaine to thy saluation amonge the Gentiles. Oh that all people would confesse thee with louing hartes, for the manifold benefites and pleasures that they haue receiued at thy hand, who dost with iustice gouerne men, and art their leader vppon

Euening

The earth; powre downe O Lord, vppon vs thy conti-nuall blessing & goodnesse, & then shall the earth yeeld vnto thy glory and prayse, and to vs fruits for meat. O God the Father, blesse vs, O God yͤ sonne, blesse vs, O God the holy Ghost blesse vs: O holy, blessed & glorious Trinitie, graunt vs thy continuall blessing, O that all the coastes of yͤ earth (Lord God) would feare and stand in awe of thee;

thee. God graunt that wee may studie to worke no man either pleasure or displeasure, but that wee may do all thinges according to thy will.

Glory be to the. &c.

As it was in the. &c.

WE looke for our Sauiour, euen the Lorde Jesus Christ, which shall change our vile body, that it may be like his glorious body, according to the power whereby hee is able to subdue all things to himselfe: saue vs O Lord waking, and kepe vs sleeping, and be so mercifull to vs, that wee may sleepe in Christ, & awake in peace. So be it.

Lord haue mercy vppon vs.

Christ haue mercy vppon vs.

Lord haue mercy vppon vs.

prayer.

VIsit wee beseech thee O lord, this our dwelling, and driue from it all the assaultes of our enemie, let thy holy Angelles dwel in it, which may kepe vs all this night in thy peace and euer let thy blessing be vppon vs: Graunt this (O most mercifull father) for thy sonnes sake, Jesu Christ, who with thee and the holy Ghost liueth and raigneth one god

O.v. world

World without end. Amen

SAue vs good Lord waking, and keepe vs ſleeping, that with Chriſt we may wake and quietly to reſt in peace.

An other Euening prayer.

MOſt mercifull and heauenly Father, I thāk thee by thy Sonne Ieſus Chriſt, that this day thou

haſt

hast giuen mee all thinges needfull both for my soule, and body, preseruing mee from all hurt and peril, I aske thee mercy for mine offences, and I most humbly beseech thee that thou wilt likewise this night keepe me from sinne and al euil, so that al my thoughts words, and workes maye please thee, I doe commit my selfe both body & soule, and all things that I goe about, into thy handes. I

beseech

Euening.

beſeech thee, that thy holy ſpirite may bee with mee, leaſt my deadly aduerſary haue any power ouer me.

A prayer at night going to bed.

THe God of Angelles & men, the founder of all creatures, viſible and inuiſible, in whoſe hand is life and death, light & darkneſſe, and al the motions of ſoule and bodye, wythout

whom

whome there is no good gift, nor perfect quietnesse of conscience, but onely vanitie and vexation of mind, and utter confusion of soul and body, and finall torments in the horrible pit of darknesse: now my Lord God, darknesse doth approch, this daye hath lost his beautie, I as unworthie of thy benefites, moste hūbly pray thee this night to blesse me, and with thy holy Angell assist mee, thy

ho-

holy spirit this night lighten me, which hast of earth
made me, and by thy crea-
tures dost nourish me, and
with thy bloud hast conse-
crated mee wyth thee too
dwell eternally in glorye,
when death hath dissolued
me, which am but vanitie.
&c. and banish Sathan frõ
mee, that neither my owne
conscience nowe vexe mee,
nor mine olde offences trou
ble mee: I most humbly
beseech thee this night to

par-

prayer.

pardon mee, which haue sore offended thee in thoght word, and deed against thy Diuine Maiestie, which sore repenteth mee: saue me good Lord, this night sleeping, from dreadfull dreame and painefull slumber deliuer me, that I maye awake in Christ, & rest in peace.

A Barker if ye will be
In name, but not in skill

Certaine godly
Sentences.

VSe inuocation on Gods holy name.

Thinke vppon the needie once a day.

The life to come, forget not.

Further the iust suite

of the poore.

Prefer Christes king dome.

Offend not in euill doing.

Set little by the iudg ment of man, but feare the iudgemēt of God.

Be at peace with all

men

men.

Vse to be acquainted with the godly.

Helpe to pacfiie displeasure.

Hastily iudge not any body.

Kill anger with pacience.

VVith pitie rebuke.

Make much of mo-
destie.
Harbour a harmeles
hart.
Let no good deede.
Speake in season.
In being well occu-
pied thinke not
long.
Loose as little time
as

as ye may.

Be alwayes one.

Fauour the friend-
lesse.

Be not vnthankfull.

Trust not the world.

Deceiue none.

Rather take hurt thã
do any.

Auenge not.

Let once bee amended.

Fauour not flatterie

Looke chiefely on your ſelfe.

Doe not forget your charge.

Let your mind bee occupied well.

Vſe pleaſures after a meane

meane.
Once you were not
here.
Away you muſt, &
turne to duſt.

FINIS.

A Barker if ye will:
In name, but not in skill.

Certaine other godly prayers.

God, thou Father, and God of my life, suffer mee neyther too haue a proud looke, nor a proud thought, turn away all voluptuousnesse from mee, let not the entisemēts of the world beguile me, let not the concupiscence of the eye deceyue mee, let not the lustes of the flesh take hold vpon mee, let not rancor & malice raigne in my heart. O lord God for thy sonne our Sauiour Jesu Christes sake, I beseech thee, that thou wilt not giue me ouer to an vnshamefast & obstinate mind. So be it.

VNto the Lord almightie, the King of mercy be now and euer eternall

nall honor and glory. Unto
the same Lord of mercy I
doe commit my soule and
body, most humbly besee=
ching thee for thy aboun=
dant mercie sake, to take ye
cure of me, & to haue mer=
cie on me. I do commit al=
so vnto thy mercy my faith
full frends and welwillers
liuing, beseeching thee to
forgiue vs all, and to haue
mercy vpon vs, and gyue
vs grace to liue according
to thy lawe, and to the glo=

cie of thy name, that we
may doe that which thou
requireſt of vs, that it will
pleaſe thee of thy mercie to
ſaue and defende vs from
all perils bodily and ghoſt=
ly, & eſpecially al thinges yͤ
ſhall turne to thy diſplea=
ſure and with all my harte
I thanke thee moſte mer=
cifull Lord, for thoſe great
benefites that thou haſte
beſtowed vppon me large=
ly in this world afore ma=
ny Creatures which are
more

more worthy a thousande
times than I: but my most
gracious Lorde, I wotte
& knowledge verely, that
all good giftes doe come
freely from thee, of thy a=
boundant mercie. Where=
fore with all my harte, I
thanke thee, and all wor=
ship, prayses, and thankes
be to thee and none other:
therefore I saye with the
prophet Dauid, Not vn=
to vs Lorde, not vnto vs,
but vnto thy name bee gi=

uen

uen all honour and glory.

An other.

ALso I commit to thy mercy mine enemies, persecutors and slaunderers, beseechinge thee to turne their hartes, and to giue vs grace one to forgiue an other from the very bottome of our hartes, that from henceforth wee may liue in loue and charitie, to thy glory, and to the in=

increase of thy kingdome.

I Do commit to thy mer=
cie thy Seruaunt oure
most gracious Queene
& this Realme, beseeching
thee to incline her harte to
all godlynesse and vertue,
that shee may long raigne
ouer vs in peace and tran=
quilitie, to liue in thy feare,
and cal vpō thy holy name,
and to be readie at al times
to sette foorth thy blessed
lawes & commaundments,
and

and that thou, O omnipo-
tent God, with thy migh-
tie hand and stretched out
arme, wilt confound al I-
dolatrie and superstition,
and set vp thy true and ho
ly religion, that thy faithfull seruants may triumph
and reioyce in thee wyth
mery hartes, and sing vn-
to thy prayse, that this the
mightie hand of God hath
brought to passe, and to thi
name giue the honour and
glorie to whom all honour

and glory is due for euer. Amen.

I Doe commit vnto thy mercie all those that in this transitory life be in sorowe, sicknesse, need, tribulation, or any other aduersitie: and specially all those that for the profession of thy Gospell and the defense of the same, doe put their liues vnto the edge of the sworde: O Lorde for thy mercies sake, forgiue them and vs our offences past, comfort them in there greuous afflictions, streg=then them in their weake=nesse, send them pacience in their tribulations, abate ÿ pride of their and our ene=mies, asswage the malice of them, confound their wic=ked deuises, that wee and they being armed with thy mightie defense, may be pre serued euermore frõ al pe=rils, to glorifie thee, which art the only giuer of al vic=

tory,

tory, through the merites of Christ. So be it.

I Do commit to thy mercie al those that do faithfully professe thy holy Gospell, beseeching thee to giue vs grace to liue according to thy lawes, that by well doing, we may stoppe the mouthes of the vngodly aduersaries of the gospell, and thereby to bring the to the right way, that we may all with one heart and one mouth glorifie thee, O Lord God, in the day of visitation, to whom all honour and glory is due: and now O my most mercifull Lord and louing father I commit vnto thy mercye my wretched soule and bodie humbly beseeching thee to haue mercy vppon mee, according to thy great and bountifull mercy.

And according to the multitude of thy tender cōpassions do away I besech thee

thee, my most greeuous ini-
quitie.

Unto God the Father, the sonne, & the holy ghost, be now and euer eternall honour and glory, world without end, Amen.

A prayer to the blessed Trinitie.

O Holy, blessed, and glorious Trinitie, three equall coeternall persons

 sons

sons and one God almighty-
tie, haue mercie vppon mee
vile abiect abhominable sin
full wretch, meekely ac=
knowledging afore thy di=
uine maiestie my long con=
tinued life in sinne, euen
from my childhode hither=
to; then good gracious
Lord, as thou giuest mee
the grace to knowledge
them, so giue me grace not
in word only but in heart
also with sorowfull con=
trition to repent and vtter

ly to forsake them: forgiue me also those sins through which by myne owne default, wicked affection and euill custome my reason is with sensualitie so blinded, as I can not discerne the for sinne. Illuminate my heart (good Lord) & geue me grace to acknowledge them: forgiue me my sins negligently forgotten, and bring them to my mynde with grace to be thorowly repentant for them: Oh mercifull God graunt mee thy grace so to dispise sinne and all worldly vanitie, that I may say wyth the blessed Apostle S. Paule: the world is crucified to me, and I to the worlde, Christ is to life, and to die is my gaine and my aduaũtage, I desire to be loosed & to be with Christ. Lord giue me thy grace to amēd my life, and to haue an eye to mine end, without any grudge, or feare of death, which to them that die in thee, is the gate of eternall life. Almightie God teach me to do thy will, take my right hand and leade mee in ẏ true way from mine, drawe me after thee, binde my mouth with snaffle and bridle when I wyll not draw unto thee. Oh gracious God, al sinfull feare, all sinfull sorowe and pensiuenesse, all sinfull hope, all sinfull mirth and gladnesse take away from mee:

on the other side concer-
ning such feare, such heaui-
nesse, such comfort, consolation and gladnesse as
shall be profitable for my
soule, doe with mee according to thy great goodnes.
O Lord giue mee grace in
all my feare and agonie to
haue recourse to that great
feare and wonderfull ago-
nie that thou my Sauiour
haddest at the Mount Oli-
uet before thy most bitter
passion, and in the meditation

tion therof to receiue ghostly comfort and consolation, profitable for my soule. Almightie God take from me al vaine glorious mindes, all appetites of my owne praise, al enuie, couetous gluttonie, sloth, and lecherie, all wrathfull affection, all appetite of reuenging, all desire of delight of other mens harms all pleasure in prouoking any person to wrath, and anger: all delight in taunting

ting or mocking any person in their affliction or trouble, and giue vnto me O Lord, an humble, quiet, peaceable, pacient, charitable, kind, tender and pitifull mind, in al my words, my workes and thoughts, to haue a tast of thy holy and blessed spirit: giue mee good Lord a full faith, and firme hope, a feruent charitie, a loue to thee, good Lord, incomparable aboue the loue of my selfe, that I

may

may loue nothing to thy diſpleaſure, but euery thing in a due order to thee. Giue me good Lord, a longing to be with thee, not for the auoyding of the calamities of this wretched worlde, nor ſo much for the auoyding of the paynes of hell, neither ſo much for the obtayning of the kingdome of heauen in reſpect of mine owne commoditie, as euen for very loue of thee: and beare me good Lorde, thy loue and fauour, whyche thing my loue to thee ward were it neuer so great, could not (but of thy great goodnes) deserue: and pardon me, good Lord, that I am so bold to aske thee so high petitiōs, being so vile and sinfull a wretch, and so vnworthy to attayne the lowest: but good Lorde, such they be as I am boūd to desire and wish, & shuld be much nerer the effectual desire of them, if my ma=

nifold

whose sinnes were not the lest, fro which O glorious trinitie, vouchsafe of thy goodnes to wash me wyth that blessed bloud that thou my swete Sauiour Iesus Christ didst shed out of thy body in the diuers torments of thy most bitter passion, that by that same grieuous passion, glorious resurrection and ascention, I may come to that unspeakable ioy, the which thou hast prepared for the

cho-

chosen and elect, through the same Jesu Christ our Saviour, to whom wyth the Father and the holy ghost, thre persons and one God, be al honour and glory world without end. So be it.

A

A contemplation of Christes Passion.

O What loue and mercie of man vndeserued from God the Father thorough his onely sonne Jesu Christ by whose flesh and bloud wee haue cleane remission of our offences. When wee call to mind this misterie of our redemption, and our sufficient sacrifice: whereby sinne, death, and hell bee put to exile, and grace mercie and peace bee obtained. For this we haue not only occasion to lament our selues, which were the very causes why Jesus did lament in care, and became poore in body, sweate water and bloud against his death, prayed in affliction, and suffred for our redemption: but also to giue dayly thankes, and to reioyce to

God

God the Father for this his sonne, by whom wee haue felowship with Angels, and are become Citizens of the Sayntes, and of the houshold of god, partakers of life for euer. O happy be they which forget not this heauenly philosophie, this giltlesse passion of Jesu Christ: to knowe and beleue this is life euerlasting and the quietnesse of conscience. This passion is our riches in pouertie, and helpe in aduersitie, and only life in death. By this his painefull affliction were al the Patriarkes, prophets, Martirs and euery beleeuing body saued that euer was or shall be, without which all flesh is damned and accursed. Now sweete Christ for this thy blessed oblation, haue mercy on mee now & in the houre of death, that in the dreadfull day of iudgment sinne, death and hell,

may

may not preuayle agaynſt mee ſinfull creature, but haue mercy vpon me accor-ding to thy greateſt mer-cie, which is this thy death and paſſion, for which bee prayſe to the holy Trini-tie for euer. Amen.

Of our frayeltie and miſerie, a Meditation or prayer.

O Miserable wretched man, that I am, how may I bee compared to any of thy Saintes that shall dwell in thy Tabernacle or holy hill, for they loue to be in holy contemplation: and I in the vaine multitude forgetting thee: they be meeke and I vnpacient: they do not forget thee, but my good lord, when do I remember thee but when affliction enforceth me, or the lamentable

fall

fall of my brethrene con=
strayne me to thanke thee:
Thou most mightie and
fearefull God of hostes, thy
holy name be blessed for e=
uer Amen. What shall I
say my god? thou art most
good and I euill, thou ho=
ly and I miserable, thou
art light and I am blind,
thou art the blessed ioye,
and I am carefull and full
of sorowe: my Lord, thou
art the Phisitian, and I
the miserable pacient: I

am nothing but vanitie &
corrupt, as euery liuing
man is. What shall I saye
(O creator) but this; that
I am thy creature, and
shall I perish: thy hands
haue made mee and were
wounded for me: thy blood
was shed for mee and hath
washed me: the holy ghost
hath satisfied me, & taught
me. yet Lord my daies are
nothing, what shoulde I
mortall man thus talke
with my selfe Lord God:

but that need hath no law: sorowe hath compelled mee to seeke comfort: sicknesse inforceth me to followe the Phisitian: conscience pricketh me to crie to thee my Lord, for a heauenly cordiall of comfort, which am in great discomfort, borne of a woman, full of miserie, and shortnesse of time, and passe away like a shadowe, neuer content wyth one estate, but in earth remain for euer. Amen.

A contemplation & prayer, exclaming of carefull passions of the soule and bodie.

WO is me carefull carkas and filthie defiled flesh, conceyued and borne in sinne, depriued of originall iustice, compared to a beast, in Adam falne as a rotten apple frō a liuing tree, what haue

I gotten by my fall: darknesse, care, miserie, affliction, sicknesse, payne, anguish, and finally dreadfull death. And alas, what shall I bee here after: a stinking carion, wormes foode, duste, and claye, poong and forsaken, rotten and consumed, blind, poore and naked, troden under the feete of my posteritie, and forgotten of all men, not knowing where my bodie is, which shall vanish niſhe like a ſhadowe, and my lyfe ſhall wyther lyke a leafe, and fade as a flower O hole G O D the more our bodies do increaſe, the nerer death doth approch, the clocke of our conſcience doth ring euery minute, the houre of death to bee at hand. Death approcheth w his ſharp dart & bloudie chariot. Away (ſayth hee) to euery liuing wight, for what is hee that ſhall not ſee death and come to nothing

thing? Oh uncertaine life, but most assured death, his net is cast ouer all fleshe, now I do reioyce, then I lament: now am I whole, then sickenesse doth come: now haue I friendes, then am I forsaken: now at libertie, soone after in bondage: now young, then age drawes nere, and thus I neuer remaine in one estate made light and proude in prosperitie, desperate in aduersitie, withered and olde

with

with care, despised in pouertie, flattered when I am in wealth, and finally vncertaine where or when I shall die. But yet I most humbly pray thee deare father for Iesus Christes sake, which suffered death for my sinnes, to haue mercie vppon me according to thy great mercy, and take not thy holy Ghost fro me, and lead me not into temptation, but deliuer me: for into thy handes I com-

mend

mend my soule thou God of truth. Amen.

A Meditation of the dreadfull day of iudgement.

O what feare and sorowe shall happen to the reprobates when they shall stand helpelesse before the terrible and dreadfull throne of God, to render accompts of all thoughtes, wordes

wordes and workes, I say the actes of the flesh and bloud in the extreeme daye when hee shall come wyth fire and then all creatures in heauen, earth, and hell, shall tremble at his presence. Then shall all guiltie consciences be opened, & euilles endlesse punished, where that iudge will not be corrupted. That daye doth come, that daye is at hande, and where as pure harts be accepted: and no

bribes

bribes of vaine giftes shall
be preferred, but Iustice
without mercie vnto the
vngodly, infernal tormets
to the wicked, endlesse care
and affliction, to the Ido=
later, fornicator, extortio=
ner, persecuter, disobedi=
ent, martherer, blasphe=
mer, theefe, false witnesse
bearer, vsurer, heretiques,
witches, and malefactors,
and to all the vessells of
reprobations, where as
shall bee heard, waylinge,

crying, lamenting, and gnaſhing of teeth, then they mourne that ſhall neuer die, hel fire neuer be quenched, nor the Iudge intreated, but the wicked ſtill moleſted with dolour, agonie, dread, and in his paine abſent from God, preſent with diuels & monſters infernall: this is the ſecond death when both body and ſoule ſhal remaine in paine as long as god is which is euerlaſting: this day is at

hand

hand, when the elect and al the Saintes, Patriarkes, Prophets, Martyrs, and all the blessed shall receyue their rewardes, not of the= selues, but onely of Jesu, before whom al the blessed shall kneele and cast off their crownes, and giue ho nour to him that sittes on the seate, whose holy name is blessed of all tonges, and kinreds, amen, amen, this is the day when all teares shalbe wiped from the face full eyes of the seruauntes of God, which shall neuer be molested, nor of worldlings be afflicted, but euerlastingly glorified with the father, the sonne, & the holy Ghost, three persons & one God, who of his mercie defend vs from damnation and that vnspeakable payne which wee thorowe sinne haue deserued euer to bee punished with all, but yet are thorow Iesus preserued, by whom we are e-

lected,

lected, redeemed, justified,
and bought frō sinne, death
and hell, to whom be laude
and prayse in the worlde
of worldes, of An=
gels and men
Amen.

An Hymne of our redeption, by Christ.

PRayse we our father louingly,
Which gently vs preserued:
When wee forsooke him wretchedly:
And by sinne death de-

serued.
His mercy was so boũ
teous,
That although we frõ
him fell,
Fréely in Christ hee
pardned vs,
And againe redéemd
vs from hell.
Glory bee to the Tri-
nitie,

The

The father, the sonne,
and spirit living:
Which art one God
and persons thrée.
To whom bee prayse
without ending.
Amen.

An Hymne or prayer to the ſonne of God.

The beamy ſunne large light doth giue,
And chaſe awaye the night.
O ſonne, O God, that alway liue,
Endue vs with thy ſpirite.

rite,
Sweete dewes from
heauen to earth god
graunt,
Of peace and quiet
mind:
That wee may serue
the liuing God,
As his statutes doe
bind.
O mightie Lord our
helpe

helpe at néede,
Driue farre away the
fœnd:
That sinne nor hel doo
vs molest,
When our life shall
make an end.
Thou art the euerla-
sting day,
That shinest in euery
place:

And

And fœdest euery li-
uing wight,
With plenteous gifts
of grace.
Into thy heauenly
hands deare God,
My spirite I doe com-
mend.
This day from sinne &
Sathans power,
Thine Angell me de-
fend.

An Hymne of the Passion of Christ.

Jesus which is the
liuely wel of wise-
dome,
And the heauenlye
truth of the father e-
ternall:
Which from heauen
to this worlde did
come,

fend.
We laud thée Father
for thy grace,
We prayſe the ſonne
which made vs frée,
We thanke the holy
ſpirite for our ſolace,
Which is one god and
perſons thrée.

An

come,
To deliuer vs thrals
from paines infer-
nall.
Of Judas was sold &
of the Jewes taken,
And of his Disciples
at midnight was for-
saken.
¶ We laud the father.
&c.

In the dawning of the
day they did him faſt
bind,
And before Pilate hee
was then conuented.
Falſe witnes againſt
Ieſus they did then
find.
When the cruel Seig-
niors in iudgement
him preſented,

Beaten was his body,
defiled was his face:
And yet God and man
the very well of
grace.
¶ We laud the father.
&c.
When thrée houres
were past befoꝛe Pi
lates trone,
All the people cried,
Kil

kil Jesus the Jewes
Kyng,
His Crowne was
thornes, in purple he
made mone.
With a crosse ouer
Cedron they did him
bring,
And prepared his dead
ly place on *Golgatha*
hill,

To suffer paines for
Adams gilt, so was
his fathers will.
¶ We laud the father.
&c.
The sixt houre appro-
ched his painfull end,
When on the trée his
body they nailed,
In heauen was his
helpe, in earth he had

no friend:
He died betwéene two théeues, on him the elders railed.
Then hée thirsted for his elect which then was in thrall,
Unthankfully they offred him Vinegar mingled with Gall.
¶ We laud the father. &c.

 This

Hymnes.

This very God, Gods
only begotten child,
Said to his Father,
why hast thou mee
forsaken?
Yet receive this sacri-
fice and my spirit un
defiled.
When the heavens
were darkened, asun
der the stones were
shaken.

shakest.
Bloud and water thē sprang from this blessed lamb.
Then graues opened the dead a liue forth came.
¶ We laud the father. &c.

Amen.

¶ *An Hymne* to God the Crea-tor.

O Creator to thée (thy creature) I call,
Who made of moulde do liue in paine:
And ſicke in ſoule my my fleſh is thrall,

Woe

Hymnes.

Woe is me, my dayes
be vaine.
Yet to God I call for
grace,
My soule in heauen to
haue place.

G.B.

¶ *An Hymne*

of the state of all Adams posteritie.

I Am the fruite of Adams hands.
Through sinne locked in Sathans bands:
Destnied to death, the childe of ire,
A flaming brand of infernall

fernall fire.
Borne I was naked &
bare,
And ſpend my time in
ſorowe and care:
And ſhall returne vn-
to the duſt,
And be depriued of car
nall luſt.
Yet thou Father didſt
Ieſus ſend,

To pardon them that
did offend.
We laud him in the
worke of might,
That we be blessed in
his sight.

¶ *An Hymne*

of the day of iudge-
ment.

SWéete Jesus of thy
mercie,
Our pitifull prayers
heare:
That wée may bée on
thy right hand,
When thou shalt ap-
peare.

For

For thou ſhalt come with heauenly power,
And ſitte on the throne.
None ſhall iudge the quicke and dead,
But thou Chriſt alone.
O Chriſt caſt vs not away in that day of ire,

ire,
When thou shalt send
before thée,
A hot consuming fire,
To purge all crea-
tures,
Defilde with Adams
sinne:
Then a new heauen &
earth,
O Lord thou wilt be-
gin.

gin.
Then the elect shal be
blessed,
Uppon thy holy hill:
But the wicked shall
be damned,
That haue withstoode
thy will.
Thy shéepe shall bée
safe,
And defended in the
fold,

fold,
The Goates shal wander,
In hunger, stormes, & colde.
The Saints shall behold thee,
In thy Throne of light:
The reprobates shall euer

B.j. Haue

Haue fearefull things
in sight.
Waylinges in wret-
chednesse,
With euerlastinge
paine:
Yet Lorde bee merci-
full,
Our liues are but
vaine.
Our fleshes shall fade

Death hath digd our graue,
Yet of thy mercie Lord,
Thy sinfull creature safe.
And blesse vs in the time of grace,
Before the daye of ire,
Whē the corrupt ele-

ments.
Shalbe purged with
fire.
We laud the father.
&c.

¶ *An other*

Hymne or prayer.

PRayse the Lord ye
servantes all,
Lift vp to hym your
handes,
The night singers in
Gods courtes,
In all christen landes.
Prayse we the Lorde
our God and kyng,
K.iij. Which

Which made the earth
and heauen,
His blessing be on vs
this night,
Which made the pla-
nets seuen.
Into thy handes, O
Lord our God,
Our soules we do com-
mend,
This night frõ sinne,
and

and Sathans pow-
er,
Thy mercy vs defend.
¶ We laud the father
for his grace. &c.

FINIS.

The Letanie.

O God the father of heauē: haue mercie vpon vs miſerable ſinners.

O God the father of heauen, haue mercy vpon vs miſerable ſinners.

O God the ſonne redemer of the worlde, haue mercie vpon vs miſerable ſinners

O God the Sonne, re-

dee-

deemer of the worlde, haue mercy vpon vs miserable sinners.

O god the holy Ghost, proceding from the father & the sonne, haue mercy vppon vs miserable sinners.

O God the holy ghost, proceeding from the father and the sonne, haue mercie vppon vs miserable sinners.

The Letanie

O holy, blessed, & glorious
Trinitie, three persons &
one God: haue mercy vpon
vs miserable sinners.

*O holy blessed and glori-
ous Trinitie, three per-
sons and one God, haue
mercie vppon us misera-
ble sinners.*

Remember not Lord our
offences, nor the offences
of our forefathers, neyther
take thou vengeance of our
sinnes

The Letanie.

sinnes, spare vs good Lord spare thy people whõ thou hast redeemed w thy most precious bloud, and be not angrie with vs for euer.

Spare vs good Lord.

From al euil and mischiefe from sinne, from the crafts and assaultes of the deuill, from thy wrath, and from euerlasting damnation.

Good lord deliuer vs.

From all blindnes of hart, from pride, vainglory, and

hypocris

hypocrisie, from enuie, hatred and malice, and al vncharitablenes.

Good Lord deliuer vs.

From fornication, and all other deadly sinne, and frō al the deceiptes of ẏ world the flesh, and the deuill.

Good lord deliuer vs.

From lightning and tempest, from plague, pestilēce and famine, from battayle and murther, and from sodaine vaine death.

Good lord deliuer vs.

From all sedition, and priuie conspiracie, fro al false doctrine and heresie, from hardnesse of hart, and contempt of thy word, & commaundement.

Good lord deliuer vs.

By the mistery of thy holy Incarnation, by thy holy Natiuitie and Circumcision, by thy Baptisme, fasting, and temptation.

Good

Good Lord deliuer vs.

By thine agony and bloudie sweate, by thy Crosse & Passion, by thy precious death and buriall, by thy glorious resurrection and ascention, and by the comming of the holy Ghost.

Good Lord deliuer vs.

In all time of our tribulation, in all tyme of our

wealth, in the houre of death, and in the daye of iudgement.

Good Lord deliuer vs.

Wee sinners doe beseeche thee to heare vs (O Lord God) & that it may please thee to rule and gouerne thy holy Church vniuersally in the right way.

Wee beseech thee to heare vs good Lord.

That it may please thee, to keepe

keepe, and strengthen in ẏ true worshipping of thee, in rightcousnesse and holinesse of lyfe, thy seruaunt Elizabeth our most gracious Queene and gouernour.

Wee beseech thee to heare vs good lord.

That it may please thee, to rule her hart in thy fayth, feare, and loue, and that she may euermore haue affiaunce in thee, & euer seeke thy honour and glory.

Wee beseech thee &c.

That it may please thee to be her defender and keper, giuing hir the victory ouer all her enemies.

Wee beseech thee &c.

That it may please thee to illuminate all Bishoppes, pastours & ministers of the Church, with true knowledge, and understandinge of thy word, and that both by their preaching and liuing they may set it foorth

and

and shew it accordingly.

Wee beseech thee &c.

That it may please thee to endue the lords of the counsaple, and all the Nobilitie with grace, wisedome and understanding.

Wee beseech thee to heare us good lorde.

That it may please thee to blesse and keepe the magistrates, giuing them grace to execute Iustice, and to maintaine truth.

Wee beseech thee to heare vs good lorde.

That it may please thee to blesse and kepe al thy people.

Wee beseech thee to heare vs good lorde.

That it may please thee to giue to all nations, vnitie, peace and concord.

Wee beseech thee to heare vs good lorde.

That it may please thee to giue

geue vs an hart to loue & dread thee, and diligently to liue after thy commaundements.

Wee beseech thee to heare vs good lorde.

That it may please thee, to giue all thy people increase of grace, to heare meekely thy woord, and to receiue it with pure affection, and to bring forth the fruites of the spirite.

Wee beseech thee to

 heare

heare vs good lorde.

That it may pleaſe thee, to bring into yͤ way of truth, all ſuch as haue erred and are deceiued.

Wee beſeech thee to heare vs good lorde.

That it may pleaſe thee, to ſtrengthen ſuch as do ſtād, and to comfort, and helpe the weake harted, and too rayſe them vp that fall, and finally to beat downe Sathan vnder our feete.

We

Wee beseech thee to heare vs good lorde.

That it may please thee, to succour, helpe and comfort all that be in daunger, necessitie, and tribulation.

Wee beseech thee to heare vs good lorde.

That it may please thee, to preserue al that trauaile by land, or by water, all women labouring of child, all sicke persons, & yong children, and to shew thy pitie vppon al prisoners & captiues.

Wee beseech thee to heare vs good lorde.

That it may please thee, to defend, and prouide for the fatherlesse children and widowes, and all that bee desolate and oppressed.

Wee beseech thee to heare vs good lorde.

That it maye please thee, to haue mercie vppon all men.

We

Wee beseech thee to heare vs good lorde.

That it may please thee, to forgeue our enemies, persecuters, and slaunderers, and to turne their hartes.

Wee beseech thee to heare vs good lorde.

That it may please thee, to geue, and preserue to our vse, the kindly fruites of the earth, so that in due time we may enioye them.

We

The Letany.

Wee beseech thee to heare vs good lorde.

That it may please thee to geue to vs true repentance to forgeue vs al our sinnes negligences & ignoraunces, and to endue vs wyth the grace of thy holy spirite, to amend our liues, according to thy holy word.

Wee beseech thee to heare vs good lorde.

Sonne of God, we besech thee to heare vs.

Sonne

Sonne of God: wee beseech thee to heare vs.

O Lambe of god, that takest away the sinnes of the world.

Graunt vs thy peace.

O Lambe of God that takest away the sinnes of the world.

Haue mercy vpon vs.

O Christ heare vs.

O Christ heare vs.

Lord haue mercy vpon vs

Lord

The Letany.

Lord haue mercy vp-
pon vs.

Christ haue mercye vpon
vs.

Christ haue mercy
vppon vs.

Lord haue mercy vppon
vs.

Lord haue mercy vp-
pon vs.

Our father which art in
heauen, &c.

And lead vs not into temp
tation.

tation.

But deliuer vs from euill.

The Versicle.

O lord, deale not with vs after our sinnes.

The Answere.

Neither reward vs after our iniquities.

Let vs pray.

O God mercifull father, that despisest not the sighing of a contrite hart, nor the desire of such as as be sorowfull, mercifullly assist our prayers that we make before thee in all our troubles and aduersities, when so euer they oppresse vs, and graciouslye heare vs, that those euilles which the craft and subtiltie of the Deuill, or man worketh agaynst vs, bee brought to nought, and by the prouidence of thy goodnes they may be dispersed, that we thy seruaunts beyng hurt by no persecution may

may euermore geue thankes to thee, in thy holy church, through Jesus christ our Lord.

O lord ariſe, helpe vs, and deliuer vs for thy names ſake.

O God, wee haue hearde with our eares, and our fathers haue declared vnto vs, the noble workes that thou didſt in their dayes, & in the old time before them.

The Letany.

O lorde arise, helpe vs, and deliuer vs for thine honor.

Glory bee to the Father, &c.

As it was in the beginning. &c.

From our enemies defend vs O Christ.

Graciously looke vppon

our

our afflictions.

Pitifully beholde the sorrowes of our hartes.

Mercifully forgiue the sinnes of thy people.

Fauourably with mercye heare our prayers.

O Sonne of Dauid haue mercy vpon vs.

Both nowe and euer, vouchsafe to heare vs, O Christ.

The Letany.

Graciously heare vs, O Christ.

Graciously heare vs, O lord Christ.

The Versicle.

O Lord let thy mercy bee shewed vpon vs.

The Answere.

As we do put our trust in thee.

Let

The Letany.

Let vs pray.

WE hūbly beseech thee O Father, mercifully to looke vpon our infirmities, and for the glory of thy names sake turne from vs those euils that wee most righteously haue deserued. And graunt that in all our troubles, we may put our whole trust & confidence in thy mercy, & euermore serue thee in holinesse, and pure-

purenesse of liuing, to thy honour and glory: through our onely mediator and aduocate Iesus Christ our Lord. Amen.

A prayer for the *Queenes Maiestie.*

O Lorde our heauenlye Father, high & mightie king of kings, lord of of Lordes; the only ruler of Princes, which doest from thy throne, beholde all the dwellers upon earth, most hartly we beseech thee with thy fauour, to beholde our most gracious soueraigne lady queen Elizabeth, and so replenishe her with the grace of thy holy spirit, that shee may alway incline too thy will, and walke in thy way. Indue hir plentifully w heauenly giftes, graunt hir in helth & wealth long ce tune, strẽgth hir that she maye vanquishe and ouer-come all her enemies: And finally after this lyfe shee may attein euerlasting ioy and feliciti: through Jesus Christ our Lorde. Amen.

A prayer for Pastors and Ministers of the Church.

ALmightie and euerlasting God, who onely workest great marvels,

uels send downe upon our
Bishops and Curates, &
al congregations commit-
ted to their charge, yͤ health
full spirit of thy grace, and
that they may truly please
thee, poure upon them the
continuall dew of thy blessing: Graunt this O lord,
for the honour of our
Aduocate & Me-
diator Jesus
Christ. A-
men.

A Prayer of Chrisostome.

ALmighty God, which hast giuen vs grace at this time with one accorde to make our cōmon supplications vnto thee, and dost promise, that when two or three be gathered together in thy name, thou wylte graūt their requestes, fulfill now, O Lord, the desi-

res

ers and petitions of thy seruauntes, as may bee moste
expedient for them, graun-
tyng vs in this worlde,
knowledge of thy trueth,
and in the worlde to come,
lyfe euerlastyng. Amen.

FINIS.

¶ *Imprinted at*
London by Henrie
Middelton, for Chri-
stopher Barker.
1574.

A Barker if ye will:
In name, but not in skill

The Queenes Prayers, or Meditations: wherein the mynde is stirred to suffer all afflictions here (*STC* 4826.6; BL shelfmark Mic.A.17425) is reproduced, by permission, from the copy at the Department of Medieval and Later Antiquities, The British Museum. The text block measures 35 × 50 mm. All signatures after F4 are missing and appear to have been removed in order to fit the text into the binding.

Words that are blotted or illegible in the original:

C3r.2 drawe
3 eternal

THE

Queenes Prayers,

Or

Meditatiōs:

Wherein the mynde is stir=red to suffer all afflic=tions here.

Colloss. iij.

If ye be risen againe vvith Christe, seeke the thinges vvhiche are aboue, vvhere Christe sitteth on the righte hande of God: set your affection on thinges that are aboue, not on thinges vvhich are on the earth.

Moste benigne Lorde Jesu, graunt me thy grace, that it maye alwaye worke in me, and perseuere with me vnto the ende.

Graunte mee, that I maye euer desire and wyll that, whiche is moste pleasaunt, and moste acceptable to thee.

Thy wyll bee my wyll, and my will bee to folowe alway thy wyll.

Lette there bee alwaye in mee one wyll, and one

desire

desire with thee, and that I haue no desire to wyll, or not to wyll, but as thou wilt.

Lorde thou knowest what thinges is most profitable, and most expedient for me.

Giue therefore what thou wilte, as muche as thou wilt, and when thou wilt.

Doe with me what thou wilt, as it shal please thee, and as shalbe most to thine honour.

Put me wher thou wilt,

and

and freely doe with me in all thinges after thy will.

Thy creature I am, and in thy handes, leade and turne me wher thou wilt.

Loe, I am thy seruaunt, ready to do al thinges that thou commaundest: for I desire not to liue to my self but to thee.

Lorde Jesus, I praye thee, graũt me grace, ẏ I neuer set my harte on the thinges of this world, but that al worldly and carnal affectiōs, may vtterly die, and be mortified in me.

Graunt mee aboue all thinges, that I may rest in thee, & fully quiet & pacifie my harte in thee.

For thou lorde arte the verie true peace of harte, and the perfecte rest of the soule: and without thee, all thinges bee greuous and vnquiet.

My lorde Jesus, I beseeche thee, bee with me in euery place, and all tymes, and let it bee to me a speciall solace, gladly for thy loue to lacke all worldlye solace.

And if thou withdrawe comforte from mee at anye time, kepe me, O lorde, frō desperation, and make mee paciently to abide thy will and ordinaunce.

O lord Iesu, thy iudgementes be righteous, & thy prouidence is muche better for me, then all that I can imagine or deuise.

Wherefore doe with me in all thinges, as it shall please thee: for it maye not be but well, all that thou doest.

If thou wylt that I be

in light, be thou blessed, if thou wilte ẏ I be in darknesse, be thou also blessed.

If thou vouchsaue to comfort me, be thou highly blessed: if thou wilt I liue in trouble, and without comforte, be thou likewise blessed.

Lord giue me grace gladly to suffer whatsoeuer thou wilte shall fall vpon me, & paciently to take it at thy hand good and bad, bitter & swete, ioye and sorowe: & for all thynges that shall

befall

befall vnto me, hartelye to thanke thee.

Keepe me lord frõ sinne and I shall thenne neither dread death nor hell.

O what thankes ought I to geue vnto thee, which haste suffered the greuous death of the crosse, to deliuer mee from my sinnes, & to obtaine euerlasting lyfe for mee.

Thou gauest vs a most perfect example of pacience fulfilling and obeyinge the wil of thy father: euen vnto the death.

Make me wretched synner obedientlye to vse my selfe after thy will in all thinges, and pacientlye to beare the burden of this corruptible life.

For thoughe this life be tedious, and as an heauye burdē to my soule: yet neuerthelesse throughe thy grace: and by example of thee, it is now made much more easye and comfortable, thenne it was before thy incarnation and passion.

Thy holy life is our way

to

to thee, and by followinge of thee, we walke to thee, ŷ art our heade and sauiour: and yet excepte thou haddest gone before, and shewed vs the waye to euerlasting life.

Who would indeuoure himselfe to followe thee? seing we be yet so slowe & dull, hauinge the lighte of thy blessed example, and holye doctrine to leade and direct vs.

O Lorde Jesu, make ŷ possible by grace, that is to me impossible by nature.

Thou knowest wel that
I maye little suffer, and ꝧ
I am anone caste downe,
and ouerthrowen wyth a
little aduersity: wherefore
I beseeche thee O Lorde,
to strengthen me with thy
spyrite, that I maye wil=
lingiye suffer for thy sake
al maner of trouble and af=
fliction.

Lord, I wil knowledge
vnto thee al mine vnrigh=
teousnes, and I will con=
fesse to the al the vnstable=
nes of my hart.

Oftentimes a verye lit=
tle

tle thing troubleth me sore and maketh mee dulle, and slow to serue thee.

And sometyme I purpose to stand strongly, but when a little trouble commeth, it is to me great anguishe and griefe, and of a right little thinge ryseth a greeuous temptation to mee.

Yea, when I thinke my selfe to be sure and strong, and that (as it seemeth) I haue the vpper hande: sodainly I feele my self ready to fall with a litle blast of temptation.

Beholde therefore good Lorde my weakenesse, and consider my frailenes beste knowen to thee.

Haue mercy on mee, and deliuer me from al iniquitye and sinne, that I be not intangled therewith.

Oftentimes it greeueth me sore, and in maner confoundeth mee, that I am so vnstable, so weake, and so fraile, in resisting sinful motions.

Whiche althoughe they draw me not away to consent, yet neuertheles their assaultes be very greuous vnto me.

And it is tedious to me to liue in such battaile, albeit I perceiue that suche battail is not profitable vnto mee.

For therby I know the better my self, & mine own infirmities, & that I must secke helpe onelye at thy handes.

O Lord God of Israel, the louer of al faythful soules, vouchsafe to behold ye labour and sorrow of mee thy

thy poore creature.

Assist mee in all thinges w^t thy grace, & so strength me with heauẽly strength, that neyther my cruel enemye the fiende, neither my wretched fleshe (which is not yet subiecte to the spirite) haue victorye or dominion ouer me.

O what a life may this bee called, where no trouble nor miserye lacketh: Where euery place is ful of snares of mortall ennemyes:

For one trouble or temptati=

tation ouerpassed, another commeth by and by, and ÿ first conflict yet duringe, a new battaile sodainly ariseth.

Wherefore Lorde Jesu, I pray thee giue mee thee grace to rest in thee aboue all thinges, and to quiete mee in thee aboue all creatures, aboue all glorye and honour, aboue all dignitye and power, aboue all cunning and policie aboue all health and beautye, aboue all riches and treasure, aboue all ioye and pleasure, aboue all fame and prayse, aboue al myrth and consolation that mans hart may take or feele besides thee.

For thou Lord God, art best, most wise, most high, most mighty, most sufficient, and most full of goodnesse, most swete, and most comfortable, moste fayre, most louinge, moste noble, most glorious, in whom al goodnesse most perfectlye is.

And therefore, whatsoeuer I haue beside thee, it is nothing to mee: For my hart may not rest, ne fullye be pacifyed, but onelye in thee.

O Lord Jesu, moste louig spouse, who shall geue me winges of perfect loue, that I may flee vppe from these worldly mysteries, & rest in thee.

O when shall I ascend to thee, and see and feele how swete thou art.

When shal I wholy gather my selfe in thee, so perfectlye, that I shal not for thy loue feele my self, thee onelye aboue my selfe, and

abone

aboue all worldly things, that thou maiest vouchsafe to visite me in such wyse, as thou dost visit thy most faithfull louers.

Now I often mourne & complaine of the myseries of this life, and with sorrowe and greate heauines suffer them.

For many thinges happen daily to me, which oftentimes trouble me, make me heauye, & darken mine understanding.

They hinder me greatlye and put my mind from

thee

thee, and so incomber mee manye wayes, ỳ I cannot freely, and clearelye desire thee, ne haue thy sweete consolations, which wyth thy blessed saintes bee alway present.

I beseeche thee, Lorde Jesu, that the sighinges, & inward desires of my hart may moue and incline thee to heare me.

O Jesu king of euerlastinge glorye, the ioye and comfort of all Christiā people, that are wandringe as pilgrimes, in the wilder-

nesse

nes of this world, my hart cryeth to thee by still desires, & my silence speaketh vnto thee, and sayth: howe long tarieth my Lord God to come to mee.

Come, O Lord, and visite mee: for withoute thee I haue no true ioye, without thee, my soule is heauy and sad.

I am in prison and bounden wyth Fetters of sorrowe, till thou O Lorde, wyth thy gracious presence vouchsafe to visite me, and to bring me again to liberty, tye, and ioye of spirite, and to shewe thy fauourable countenaunce vnto mee.

Open my hart lord, that I may beholde thy lawes, and teache me to walke in thy commaundements.

Make me to knowe and folow thy wil, and to haue alwaies in my remēbraūce thy manifold benefits that I may yeld due thankes to thee for them.

But I knowledge and confesse for truthe, that I am not able to geue the cō-digne thanckes of the least bene-

benefite thou haste geuen mee.

O Lorde all giftes and vertues, that any mā hath in bodye or soule, naturall, or supernatural, be thy giftes, and come of thee, and not of oure selfe, and they declare the great riches of thy mercye and goodnesse vnto vs.

And thoughe some haue moe giftes then other, yet they all procede from thee, and without thee, the least cannot be had.

O Lord, I accompt it for

a great benefit, not to haue many worldly gifts, wherby the laude and praise of men might blind my soule and deceiue mee.

Lord, I know ỳ no man ought to be abashed, or miscontent, that he is in a low estate in this world, & lacketh the pleasures of this life: But rather to be glad and reioyce thereat.

For so muche as thou haste chosen the poore and meeke persons, & suche as are despised in the worlde, to be thy seruauntes, and familiar frendes.

Witnesse bee thy blessed Apostles, whō thou madest chiefe Pastours, and spyrituall gouernours of thy flocke, which departed frō the counsaile of ÿ Iewes, reioysinge that they were compted worthye to suffer rebuke for thy name.

Euen so O Lord, graūt that I thy seruaunt maye be as wel content to be taken as the leaste, as other be to be greatest, and that I be as well pleased to be in the lowest place, as in ÿ high-

highest, and as glad to bee of no reputation in the worlde for thy sake, as other are to be noble and famous.

Lord, it is the worke of a perfect man, neuer to sequestre his minde frō thee, and among many worldlye cares to go withoute care: not after the maner of an idle or a dissolute personne, but by the prerogatiue of a free minde, alwaye minding heauenly things, and not by inordinate affection to any creature.

I beseech thee therefore my Lorde Jesu, keepe mee from yͤ superfluous cares of this worlde, that I bee not inquieted with bodily necessityes, ne that I bee not taken with the volup=tuous plesures of yͤ world ne of the fleshe.

Preserue mee from all thinges whiche hinder my soules healthe, that I bee not ouerthrowen wythe them.

O Lord God, which art sweetenes, vnspeakable, turne into bitternes to me,

all

all worldly and fleshly desires, which might drawe me from the loue of eternal things, to the loue of short and vile pleasure.

Let not fleshe and bloud ouercome mee, ne yet the worlde, wyth hys vaine glorye deceiue mee, nor the feinde, with his manifolde craftes supplante mee: But geeue mee Ghostlye strength in resisting them, pacience in suffering them, and constancye in perseuering to the end.

Giue me for all worldlye

lye delectacions, the most sweete consolacion of thy holy spyrit, & for al fleshly loue indue my soule wyth feruent loue of thee.

Make mee stronge inwardlye in my soule, and cast out thereof all vnprofitable cares of this world that I be not ledde by vnstable desires of earthlye thinges, but that I maye repute all thinges in this world (as they be) transitorye, and sone vanishinge awaye and my selfe also with theim, drawinge toward mine ende.

For nothinge vnder the Sūne may long abide, but all is vanity, and affliction of spirit.

Geue mee Lorde, therefore heauenlye wisedome, that I may learne to seeke and finde thee, and aboue all thinges, to loue thee.

Giue me grace to withdrawe me, from them that flatter me, and paciently to suffer them, that vniustlye greue me.

Lorde, when temptation or tribulation commeth,

vouchſafe to ſuccoure me,
that all maye tourne to my
ghoſtly comfort, and paci=
ently to ſuffer, and alwaye
to ſaye, thy name be bleſ=
ſed.

Lorde, trouble is nowe
at hande, I am not well,
but I am greatly vexed &
this preſent affliction. O
moſte glorious Father,
what ſhal I doe? Anguiſh
and trouble are on euerye
ſyde, helpe now I beſecch
thee in this houre, thou
ſhalt be lauded and praiſed
when I am perfectly made

meeke

meeke before thee, and whē I am clearelye deliuered by thee.

May it therefore please thee to delyuer mee, for what may I most sinfull wretche doe? Or whither may I goe for succour but to thee?

Geeue me pacience nowe at this time in al my trouble, helpe mee, Lord God, & I shal not feare ne dread what troubles soeuer shal fall vppon mee.

And nowe what shal I saye,

saye, but that thy will bee done in mee: I haue deserued to be troubled and greued: and therefore it behoueth, that I suffer as long as it pleaseth thee.

But would to God that I might suffer gladly, till the furious tempests were ouerpassed, and that quietnes of hart might come againe.

Thy mightye hande O Lorde, is stronge enoughe to take this trouble from mee, and to asswage ye cruell assaultes thereof, that

I

I bee not ouercome wyth them, as thou haste oftentimes don before this time, that when I am clearelye deliuered by thee, I maye with gladnes saye: the right hande of him that is highest, hath made thys chaunge.

Lord graunt me thy singuler Grace, that I maye come thether, wher no creature shall let mee, ne keepe me from the perfect beholding of thee.

For as long as any transitorye thinge keepeth mee backe,

backe, or hath rule in mee, I maye not freely ascende to thee.

O Lord without thee, nothing may long delite or please: for if anye thinge should be lyking & sauourie, it must be through help of thy grace, seasoned with the spice of thy wisedome.

O euerlasting light, far passinge all thinges, sende downe the beames of thy brightnesse from aboue, and purifye and lighten the inwarde partes of my hart.

Quic-

Quicken my soule, and all the powers thereof, that it maye cleaue fast, and bee ioyned to thee in ioyfull gladnesse of ghostly rauishinges.

O whē shall that blessed houre com, that thou shalt visit me, and glad me with thy blessed presence, when thou shalte be to mee all in all: verely vntil that time come, ther can be no perfect ioy in mee.

But alas, mine old mā, that is in my carnall affections liue stil in mee, and are

are not crucifyed, nor perfectly dead.

For yet striueth the flesh against the spirit, and moueth great battel inwardly against me, and suffreth not thy kyngdome of my soule to liue in peace.

But thou good Lorde, that hath the Lordship ouer al, and power of the Sea, to asswage the rage, and surges of the same, arise, and helpe mee, destroye the power of myne ennemyes, which alwayes make battaile againste mee, shewe

forth

forth the greatnes of thy goodnes, and let the power of thy right hand be glorifyed in mee. For there is to me none other hope nor refuge, but in thee only my Lord, my God: to thee bee honour and glorye euerlasting.

O Lord, graunt me, that I may wholye resigne my selfe to thee, and in all thinges to forsake my self, and paciently to bere my crosse and to follow thee.

O Lord, what is man, ẏ thou vouchsauest to haue

mind of him, & to visit him

Thou art alway one, alway good, alway righteous & holy, iustly & blessedly disposing al thinges after thy wisedome.

But I am a wretch, and of my selfe alwaye readye, and prone to euill, and doe neuer abide in one state, but many times do varie & chaunge.

Neuerthelesse it shal be better wyth mee, when it shall please thee: for thou, O Lorde onelye arte hee, that maiest helpe mee, and

thou

thou maiest so confirme, & stablishe me, that my harte shall not be chaunged from thee, but be surely fixed, & finally rest, and be quieted in thee.

I am nothing els of my self but vanitie before thee an unconstaunt creature, & a feeble: & therefore, wherof may I rightfully glorie? Or why shoulde I looke to be magnified?

Who so pleaseth him self without thee, despiseth thee: and he that deliteth in mens prayses, looseth

The true praise before thee.

The true prayse is to be praised of thee: and the true ioye is to reioyce in thee.

Wherefore thy name (O lorde) be praysed, and not myne.

Thy workes be magnified and not myne, and thy goodnesse be alwayes lauded and blessed.

Thou arte my glorie, & the ioye of my hart, in thee shall I glorie and reioyce, and not in my selfe, nor in any worldly honour or dignitie, whiche to thy eternal nall glory compared, is but a shadowe and a very vanitie.

O lorde, we liue here in great darkenesse, and are sone deceiued with the vanities of this worlde, and are soone greeued with a litle trouble, yet if I could beholde my selfe well, I should plainly see, ẏ what trouble soeuer I haue suffered, it hath iustly comen vpon mee, bicause I haue ofte sinned, and greeuously offended thee.

To me therfore be confukon and despite is due: but to thee laude, honour, and glorie.

Lorde sende me helpe in my troubles, for mās help is little worthe.

Howe often haue I been disappoincted, where I thought I shold haue foūd frendship: And how often haue I founde it, where as I least thought:

Wherefore it is a vaine thing to truste in man: for the true truste and healthe of man is onely in thee.

Blessed bee thou lorde ther=

therefore, in all thinges ÿ happeneth vnto vs, for we be weake & vnstable, sone deceiued, and sone chaunged from one thinge to an other.

O lord God most righteous iudge, strong, & pacient, whiche knowest the frailtie, and malice of man, be thou my whole strẽgth and comfort in all necessities: for myne owne conscience (lord) sufficeth not. Wherfore, to thy mercie I dooe appeale, seing no man may be iustified, ne ap

 peare

peare ryghteous in thy sight, if thou examine hym after thy/iustice.

O blessed mantion of thy heauenly citie, O most cle=rest day of eternitie, whom the nyghte maye neuer darken.

This is the daye alway cleare and mearie, alwaye sure, and neuer chaunging his state.

Would to God this daye might shortly appeare, and shine vpō vs, and that this worldly phantasies were at an ende.

This daye shineth clearely to thy Sainctes in heauen with euerlastinge brightnesse, but to vs pilgrimes in earth, it shineth obscurely, and as through a mirrour or glasse.

The heauenly citezeins knowe howe ioyous this daye is: but we outlawes, the children of Eue, wepe and wayle the bitter tediousnesse of our daye, that is, of this present life, short and euill, full of sorow and anguishe.

Where man is oftẽtimes

defiled with sinne, encom-
bred with affliction, inquieted with troubles, and
wrapped in cares, busied
with vanities, blynded
with errours, ouercharged
with laboures, vexed with
tẽptatiõs, ouercome with
vaine delites, & pleasures
of the worlde, & greuously
tormented with penurie &
neede.

O, when shall the ende
come of all these miseries?

When shall I be clearely
deliuered from the bõdage
of synne.

When

When shal I (lorde) haue onely mynde on thee, and fully be glad and merie in thee.

When shall I bee free without letting, and bee in perfecte libertie, without griefe of body and soul.

When shal I haue peace without trouble: peace within and without: and on euery side stedfast and sure?

O Lorde Jesu, when shall I stande and beholde thee: and haue full sighte & contẽplation of thy glory?

When

When shalt thou bee to me all in all? And when shall I be with thee in thy kingdome that thou haste ordeyned for thyne electe people frō the beginning?

I am lefte here poore, & as an outlawe, in the land of myne ennemies, where daily be battailes, & great misfortunes.

Comforte mine exile, asswage my sorowe, for all my desire is to be with the.

It is to me an vnpleasaunt burden, what pleasure soeuer the worlde offreth me here.

I deſire to haue inward fruition in thee, but I can not attaine thereto.

I couet to cleaue faſte to heauenlye thynges, but worldly affections, plucke my mynde downeward.

I would ſubdue al euill affections, but they daylye rebell and ryſe againſt me, and will not be ſubiect vnto my ſpirite.

Thus I wretched creature fight in my ſelfe, and am greeuous to my ſelfe, whyle my ſpirite deſireth to be vpwarde and contrary my fleshe draweth mee downwarde.

O, what suffer I inwardly? I goe about to mynde heauenly thinges, and straight a great rable of worldly thoughtes rush into my soule.

Therfore, Lorde, be not long awaye, ne depart not in thy wrath from me.

Sende me the lighte of thy grace, destroye in mee all carnall desires.

Sende forthe the hotte flames of thy loue, to burn

and

and consume the cloudye phantasies of my minde.

Gather, O Lorde, my wittes and the powers of my soule together in thee, and make me to despyse all worldly thinges, and by thy grace strongly to resist and ouercome all motions and occasions of sinne.

Help me, thou euerlasting truthe, that no worldly gile, nor vanitie hereafter, haue power to deceiue me.

Come also, thou heauenly sweetenes, & let all bitternes of sinne flee farre from

from me.

Pardon me, and forgiue me as ofte as in my praier, my mynde is not surelye fixed on thee.

For many tymes I am not there, where I stande, or sitte: But rather there, whether my thoughtes carie mee.

For there I am, where my thoughtes bee, and there as customablie is my thought, there is that, that I loue.

And that oftentimes cōmeth into my minde, that by

by custome pleased me best, and that deliteth me moste to thinke vpon.

Accordingly as thou doest saye in thy Gospell: where as a mans treasure is, ther is his harte.

Wherefore if I loue heauen, I speake gladly therof, and of suche thinges as be of God, and of that, that appertaineth to his honor, and to the glorifying of his holy name.

And if I loue the world, I loue to talke of worldlye thinges, and I ioye anone

in worldly felicitie, and sorrowe and lament soone for
worldly aduersitie.

If I loue the fleshe, I
imagine oftentimes that,
that pleaseth the fleshe.

If I loue my soule, I
delite muche to speake, and
to heare of thinges, that be
for my soules health.

And whatsoeuer I loue,
of that I gladly heare, and
speake, & beare the images
of them still in my mynde.

Blessed is that man, that
for the loue of the Lorde,
setteth not by ỷ pleasures

of this worlde, and lear=
neth truly to ouercome him
selfe, and with the fauour
of the spirite, crucifieth his
fleshe, so that in a cleane &
a pure conscience, he maye
offer his prayers to thee, &
be accepted to haue compa=
ny of thy blessed Angels,
all earthly thinges exclu=
ded from his harte.

Lorde, and holy father,
be thou blessed nowe and
euer: for as thou wilte, so
is it doone, and that thou
doest, is alwaye beste.

Lette me thy humble &

vnworthy seruaunte, ioye onely in thee, and not in my self, ne in any thing els beside thee.

For thou lorde, art my gladnes, my hope, my croune, and all my honour.

What hath thy seruaunt, but that he hath of thee, & that without his deserte?

All things be thine, thou hast created and made thẽ.

I am poore, and haue been in trouble and payne, euer from my youthe, and my soule hath ben in great heauines thorowe mani-

folde

folde passions, that come of the worlde, and of the fleshe.

Wherefore (Lorde) I desyre that I may haue of thee, the ioye of inwarde peace.

I aske of thee, to come to that reste, whiche is ordeined for thy chosen children, that be vsed and nourished with the lighte of heauenlye comfortes: for without thy helpe, I can not come to thee.

Lorde gyue mee peace, giue me inward ioye, and

then my ſoule ſhalbe ful of heauenly melody, and bee deuoute, and feruent in thy laudes and prayſinges.

But if thou withdrawe thy ſelfe from me (as thou haſte ſometyme done) then maye not thy ſeruaunte runne the waye of thy cōmaundementes, as I did before.

For it is now with me, as it was, when the Lanterne of thy ghoſtly preſence, did ſhyne vpon my head, and I was defended vnder the ſhadowe of thy

wynges

wynges from all perilles and daungers.

O mercifull Lorde Jesu, euer to be praysed, the tyme is come, that thou wilt proue thy seruaunte, and rightfull is it, that I shall nowe suffer somewhat for thee.

Now is the howre come, that thou hast knowen frō the beginning, that thy seruaunt for a tyme shoulde outwardlye bee sette at naught, and inwardly to leane to thee.

And that he should bee

despised in the sight of the worlde, and be brokẽ with afliction, that he may after aryse with thee in a newe light, and be clarified, and made glorious in the kingdome of heauen.

O holy father, thou hast ordeined it so to bee, and it is doen as thou hast cõmaunded.

This is thy grace (O Lorde) to thy friende, to suffer him to bee troubled in this worlde for thy loue, howe often soeuer it bee, & of what persone soeuer it bee, vee, and in what maner so euer thou wilt suffer it to fall vnto him: for without thy wyll or sufferaunce, what thing is done vpon the earth?

It is good to mee (O lord) that thou hast mekekened me, that I may ther by learne to knowe thy righteous iudgementes, & to put from mee all maner of presumption and statelinesse of harte.

It is very profitable for me that confusion hath couered my face, that I may learne thereby rather to seke to thee for helpe and succour, then to man.

I haue thereby learned to dread thy secret and terrible iudgementes, whiche scourgeste the righteous with the synner, but not without equitie & iustice.

Lorde, I yelde thankes to thee, that thou haste not spared my sinnes, but hast punished me with scourges of loue, and haste sent me afflictiō and anguishes within and without.

No creature vnder hea-

uen

uen may comforte mee, but thou (Lord God) the heauenly leache of mās soule, which strikest and healest, which bringest a man nigh unto death, & after restorest him to life againe, that he may thereby learne to knowe his owne weakenesse and imbesilitie, and the more fully to truste in thee (Lorde.)

Thy discipline is layde upon me, and thy rodde of correction hath taught me, and under that rodde I wholy submitte me.

Strike

Strike my backe & my bones, as shall please thee, and make me to bowe my croked will, vnto thy wil.

Make mee a meeke and an humble disciple, as thou haste sometime doen with me, that I may walke after thy will.

To thee I committe my selfe to be corrected: for better it is to be corrected by thee here, then in tyme to come.

Thou knowest al things and nothing is hidde from thee, that is in mans conscience.

Thou

Thou knowest al things to come before they fal, and it is not nedefull, that any man teache thee, or warne thee of any thing that is done vpon the earth.

Thou knowest what is profitable for me, and how muche tribulations helpen to purge away the ruste of synne in me.

Do with mee after thy pleasure, I am a synfull wretche, to none so well knowen as to thee.

Graunt me (lorde) that to knowe, that is necessary

to be

to be knowen: that to loue, that is to be loued: that to desire, that pleaseth thee: that to regarde, that is precious in thy sight: and that to refuse, that is vyle before thee.

Suffer me not to iudge thy misteries after my outwarde sences, ne to gyue sentence after the hearing of the ignoraunte, but by true iudgement to discerne thinges spirituall: and aboue all thinges, alway to searche, and followe thy wyll and pleasure.

O lorde Jesu, thou arte all my richesse, and all that I haue, I haue it of thee.

But what am I (lorde) that I dare speake to thee? I am thy poore creature, & a worme moste abiecte.

Beholde Lorde, I haue nought, and of my selfe I am noughte worthe, thou art only God, righteous & holye, thou orderest all thinges, thou giueste all thinges, and thou fulfillest al things with goodnesse.

I am a sinner, barren & voyde of godly vertue.

Re-

Remember thy mercies, and fil my harte with plētie of thy grace, for thou wilt not that thy workes in me, ſhould be in vaine.

Howe may I beare the miſerie of this life, excepte thy grace and mercy doe comfort me:

Tourne not thy face frō me, deferre not the viſiting of mee, ne withdrawe not thy comfortes, leaſt happely my ſoule be made as drie earth without the water of grace.

Teache me lorde to fulfill thy

fill thy

fill thy will, to liue mekely, & worthely before thee, for thou arte all my wysedome and cunning, thou art he that knowest me as I am, that knowest me before the world was made, and before I was borne, or brought into this life, to thee (O Lord) be honour, glorie, and prayse for euer and euer. Amen.

Laus deo inæternum.

Amen.

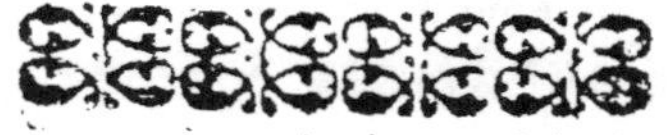

A deuoute prayer to be sayde daiely.

O Almighty & eter-
nall God, whiche
vouchsauest y^t wee
as it were heauen-
ly chyldren, should euerye
one of vs cal thee our heauenly father: Graunt that
emong vs be purenesse, and
example of innocent lyfe,
thy moste holy name maye
be sanctified, that all other
nations, beholdynge oure
goodnesse & vertuous de-
des, that thou woorkest in

vs,

vs, may be styrred to hallow and glorifye thee.

Graunt (O Lord) that the kingdome of thy grace and mercye, may reigne cōtinually in our harts, so yͤ wee maye be worthye to be partakers of the realme of glorye and maiestye.

Graūt that vnto the very death, wee refuse not to followe thy deuine will, that wee accordinge to the example of the celestial citezens, agreeing together quietly vnited in spirit, all controuersye in opinions layed apart, the lustes of ye flesh being subdued, and ye flatteringe assaultes of the world and the deuill ouercom, neuer wrastel against thy most holy will, but obeye it in all thinges.

Graunt (O Lord) for our bodye needefull sustenãce, that we may the more freelye serue thee. Geeue vs, we beseech thee (O merciful father) that heauenlye breade, the bodye of thy sonne Iesu Christ, the very foode and health of our soules: giue vs the breade of thi diuine preceptes, that we may trulye walke, and liue after them.

Giue vs the bread of the heauenly worde, which is thy stronge buttresse, and sure defence of our soules, that we being wel fedde, & filled with this foode, may worthily come to the celestiall feast where as is no hunger.

Graūt (O Lord) ẏ we paciently beare and suffer our enemyes, and such as hurt vs, and willinglye to forgiue the offences committed againſt vs, that ſoe we may finde thee Lord in forgiuing vs oure treſpaſſes, milde and mercifull.

Graunte O Lorde, that we be not vtterly ledde into temptation, that therby we ſhould be loſt: but in al perilles of temptation, & in the middes of the ſtormy tempeſtes and tribulations, let vs thy children, perceyue and feele thy fatherlye ſuccoure, readye to helpe vs, leaſt that we (ouercome with the naughty craftes, and deceipts of the temptour) shoulde be drawen into euerlastinge destruction: but when we be wel assayed, approued, and pourged with the fyre of temptation, then let vs finish our course, and so wel and valiauntly fighte, that we may for euermore, liue with thee in that heauenlye Cittye, where and against thee, which no maner tẽptation can preuaile. Finally, graunt most merciful father, ỷ we, through thy benigne goodnes, may be deliuered from all euils

Preſente, and to come, both of body and ſoule, and that at the laſt, the yoke of the foule feinde beinge ſhaken of, we may poſſeſſe the heritage of the Heauenlye kingdom: which thi ſonne, with hys precious bloude bought for vs thy childrē; and therefore euer to haue the fruition of celeſtial delectations, accompanyed with Angelles and bleſſed ſainctes, through the help, benignitye, & grace of our Sauiour Jeſus Chriſte, to whom, and to thee oure father,

father, & to ẏ holy Ghoste, be glory and honor, now and euer. Amen.

The Letanye.

O GOD the father of heauē, haue mercye uppon us myserable sinners.

O God the father. &c.

O God the sonne redemer of the world, haue mercye uppon us myserable sinners.

O God the sonne. &c.

O God yͤ holy ghost, proceding from the father and the sonne haue mercy vpon vs miserable sinners.

O God yͤ holy ghost. &c.

O holye, blessed, and glorious Trinitye. three personnesa nd one God, haue mercye vpon vs miserable sinners.

O holy, blessed, &c.

Remember not Lord oure offences, nor the offences of oure forefathers, neyther take thou vengeance of our sinnes, spare vs good lord,

spare

The ‘Kalender’ (BL shelfmark Mic.A.17425) is reproduced, by permission, from the copy at the Department of Medieval and Later Antiquities, The British Museum. The text block measures 35 × 50 mm. This copy is missing all signatures before A2 and after B7.

Words that are blotted or illegible in the original:

A4v.2 The Moone xxx.
   12 Aries
A6v.13 Sun in gem
B3v.16 sun in Scor

For .xx. yeare.

The number of yeares.	Easter.	Golden number.	Dom. letter.	Leape yeare.
1583	31. Mar.	7	F	
1584	19. April	8	E	D
1585	11. April.	9	C	
1586	3. April.	10	B	
1587	16. April.	11	A	
1588	7. April.	12	G	F
1589	30. Mar.	13	E	
1590	19. April.	14	D	
1591	4. April.	15	C	

The kalender.

January hath.xxxj.dayes.

The Moone.xxx.

19 A New yeares day. j
8 b Oct of Step. ij
c Oct of John iij
16 d Oct of Innoc. iiij
5 e Depos.of Edw. v
f The Epiphanie vj
13 g Felix & Janu. vij
2 A Luci. & his fe. viij
b Joyce virgin ix
10 c [illegible] x
d Paule first Her. xj
18 e Archade martir xij
7 f Hylarie bishop xiij
g Felix preest xiiij

15 Isydore mar. xv
4 b Marcel. mar. xvj
c Depo. of Anto. xvij
12 d Prisce virgin. xviij
1 e Wolston bisshop xix
f Fabian & Seb. xx
9 g Agnes virgin xxj
Vincent mar. xxij
17 b Timothe disc. xxiij
6 c Macari abbot xxiiij
d Con. of Paule xxv
14 e Policarp bish. xxvj
3 f Juliā bisshop xxvij
g Chrisost. doc. xxviij
11 Valere bish. xxix
b Batild Quee. xxx
19 c Satur. & Vic. xxxj

February hath.xxviij.dais

The Moone.xxix.

8	d	Fast.	j
	e	Puri of Mary.	ij
16	f	Blase bishop.	iij
5	g	Gilbert confes.	iiij
	A	Agathe virgin	v
13	b	Veda. & Aman.	vj
2	c	Dorothe virg.	vij
	d	Sun in pisces	viij
10	e	Angule virgin	ix
	f	Paule bishop.	x
18	g	Appoline virgin	xj
7	A	Eulalie	xij
	b	Eufrase virgin	xiij
15	c	Wolfrane bish.	xiiij

4	d	Valen mar.	xv
	e	Julian virg in	xvj
12	f	Policron bish.	xvij
1	g	Simion mar.	xviij
	A	Julian bishop	xix
9	b	S. Mildred	xx
	c	Sabin & Juli.	xxj
17	d	Cathedra	xxij
6	e	Fast.	xxiij
	f	Math apost.	xxiiij
14	g	69 martyrs	xxv
3	A	Peters chayre	xxvj
	b	Alexander bi.	xxvij
11	c	Oswald bish.	xxviij

March hath.xxxj.dayes.

The Moone xxx

19	d	Dauid bishop	j
8	e	Martine	ij
	f	Chad bishop	iij
16	g	Gilbert confes.	iiij
5	a	Focas and Euse.	v
	b	Victor & Victo.	vj
13	c	Perpet. & Fel.	vij
2	d	Apoline mar.	viij
	e	Agathe virgin	ix
10	f	Gregorie bishop	x
8	g	Sunne in Aries	xj
	a	S. Gregorie	xij
17	b	Theodore mar.	xiij
	c	Peter martyr.	xiiij

15	d	Longine mar.	xv
4	e	Quirine mar.	xvj
	f	Gertrude vir.	xvij
12	g	Edward king	xviij
1	[illegible]	Jos. Mar. hus.	xix
	b	Cutbert bishop	xx
9	c	Benedict abbot	xxj
	d	Isodose bish.	xxij
17	e	Theod. priest	xxiij
6	f	Fast	xxiiij
	g	Anun. of [illegible]	xxv
14	[illegible]	Castor martir	xxvj
3	b	Ludger bish.	xxvij
	c	Dorothe vir.	xxviij
11	d	Victorine	xxix
	e	Sabine virgin	xxx
19	f	Joceline bishop	xxxj

Aprill hath.xxx.dayes.

The Moone.xxix.

13	g	Theodore vir.	j
16	A	Mary egip.	ij
5	b	Richard bischop	iij
	c	Ambrose bisch.	iiij
13	d	Martian & mar.	v
2	e	Sextus mar	vj
	f	Eufamine vir.	vij
10	g	Dionisius	viij
	A	Perpetuus bi.	ix
18	b	Passio virgin	x
7	c	Son in Taur.	xj
	d	Appolin mar.	xij
25	e	Sother martir	xiij
4	f	Tyburt mar.	xiiij

	g	Oswald bishop	xv
12	A	Isydore bishop	xvj
1	b	Anecete bish.	xvij
	c	Eleuther bish.	xviij
9	d	Hermogines	xix
	e	Alphege	xx
17	f	Quintine	xxj
6	g	Clete bishop	xxij
	A	George mar.	xxiij
14	b	Wilfride conf.	xxiiij
3	c	Mark euan.	xxv
	d	Clete confes.	xxvj
11	e	Anast. bishop	xxvij
	f	Vitalis mar.	xxviij
19	g	Peter of Mil.	xxix
8	A	Dep. of Erken.	xxx

May hath.xxxj.dayes.

The Moone.xxx.

	b	Philip & Jacob.	j
16	c	Athanasius	ij
5	d	Finding the cro.	iij
	e	Edward archb.	iiij
13	f	John Portlatin	v
2	g	John Beuerley	vj
	A	Appea. of Mich.	vij
10	b	Transl. of Nic.	viij
	c	Gordian.	ix
18	d	Anthonie mar.	x
7	e	[illegible]	xj
	f	Pancrace mar.	xij
15	g	Seruatius bish.	xiij
4	A	Boniface mar.	xiiij

The kalender.

b Isydore mar. xv
12 c Brandt.bish. xvj
1 d Trans. Barn, xvij
e Diosco.mar. xviij
9 f Donati bishop xix
g Dunston conf. xx
17 Barnardine xxj
6 b Helene Quene xxij
c Desedero mar. xxiij
14 d Julian virg. xxiiij
3 e Desidere mar. xxv
f Adelme confes. xxvj
11 g Augustin con. xxvij
Germain ma. xxviij
19 b Petronil. vir. xxix
8 c Corone martir xxx
16 d Felix bishop xxxj

The kalender.

June hath .xxx. dayes.

The Moone .xxx.

	e	Nicome mar.	j
5	f	Marcelline	ij
	g	Erasmus mar.	iij
13	A	Petrocius con.	iiij
2	b	Boniface bish.	v
	c	Mellonis bish.	vj
10	d	Medard & Gil.	vij
	e	Trans. Edm.	viij
18	f	yuon confessor	ix
7	g	Anthonie	x
	A	Barnabie apo.	xj
15	b	Sun in Can.	xij
4	c	Tran. Wal.	xiij
	d	Basilides con.	xiiij

The kalender

12	e	Vite modeste	xv
1	f	Tran. Richard	xvj
	g	Botolph conf.	xvij
6	a	Marc. & Ma.	xviij
	b	Geruasius ma.	xix
27	c	Tran. Edw.	xx
6	d	walburge virg.	xxj
	e	Albane martir	xxij
14	f	Fast	xxiij
3	g	Nat. Jo. Ba.	xxiiij
	a	Tran. Eleg.	xxv
11	b	John & Paul.	xxvj
	c	Crescens	xxvij
19	d	Fast	xxviij
8	e	Peter & Paul.	xxix
16	f	Com. of Paul.	xxx

July hath.xxxi.dayes.

The Moone.xix.

5	g	Octa.of John	i
	a	Visita.of Mary	ij
13	b	Transl.of Tho.	iij
2	c	Tran.of mar.	iiij
	d	Zoe virgin	v
10	e	Octa.of Peter	vj
	f	Depo.of Grim.	vij
18	g	Cirill bishop	viij
7	a	Dog day beg.	ix
	b	Seuen brethren	x
15	c	Tran of Bene.	xj
4	d	Priuate mar.	xij
	e	Tra.of Benet	xiij
12	f	Sun in Leo.	xiiij

1	g	Tran. of Swit.	xv
	A	Tran. Osmond	xvj
9	b	Kelome king	xvij
	c	Arnulph mar.	xviij
17	d	Ruffin & Just.	xix
6	e	Margaret vir.	xx
	f	Praxede martir	xxj
14	g	Mary Mag.	xxij
3	A	Apolina. ma.	xxiij
	b	Fast.	xxiiij
11	c	James apo.	xxv
	d	An. mo. of ma.	xxvj
19	e	Seuē slepers	xxvij
7	f	Sampson bi.	xxviij
16	g	Felix & his fel.	xxix
5	A	Abdon & Sen.	xxx
	b	German bish.	xxxj

August hath.xxxj.dayes.

The Moone xxx.

13	c	Lammas day	j
2	d	Stephen bishop	ij
	e	Inuen of Ste.	iij
10	f	Iustine priest	iiij
	g	Festum niuis.	v
18	[illegible]	Transfi.of chri.	vj
7	b	Feast of Iesus	vij
	c	Ciri.& his fel.	viij
15	d	Romain mar.	ix
4	e	Laurence mar.	x
	f	Tiburt.mar.	xj
12	g	Clare virgin	xij
1	[illegible]	Hyppolite	xiij
	b	Sun in Vir.	xiiij

6 c Assum of Ma. xv
d Rocke mar. xvj
17 e Oct. of Lau. xvij
6 f Dog day ende xviij
g Magnus mar. xix
13 A Barnard con. xx
3 b Lewes confes. xxj
c Oct. assump. xxij
11 d Fast. xxiij
19 e Bartho. apo. xxiiij
f Lewes king. xxv
8 g Severn bish. xxvj
16 A August. conf. xxvij
b Ruffe mart. xxviij
5 c Johns behed. xxix
d Felix & Auda. xxx
13 e Cuth. virgin xxxj

The kalender.

Septẽber hath .xxx. dayes.

The Moone .xxix.

11	f	Giles abbot	j
	g	Anthonie martir	ij
10	A	Ordin Grego.	iij
	b	Tran. of Ceth.	iiij
18	c	Bertini abb.	v
7	d	Eugeny confes.	vj
	e	Enurcius bish.	vij
25	f	Natiuitie Ma.	viij
4	g	Gorgonij mar.	ix
	A	Siluius bish.	x
19	b	Proth. & Iacint	xj
1	c	Martinian	xij
	d	[illegible]	xiij
9	e	Maurilius.	xiiij

f Holy crosse. xv
17 g Edith virgin. xvj
6 Lambert mar. xvij
b Vict. & Coro. xviij
14 c Januarie mar. xix
3 d ¶ Fast xx
e Mathewe apo. xxj
11 f Mauricius xxij
19 g Tecla virgin xxiij
Andoch. mar. xxiiij
8 b Firmine bish. xxv
c Ciprian & Ju. xxvj
16 d Cosme & Da. xxvij
5 e Exupere xxviij
13 f Michael arch. xxix
2 g Hierom prest xxx

October hath.xxxj. dayes.

The Moone.[illegible]

		Remege bishop	j
10	b	Leodegare mar.	ij
	c	Candide mar.	iij
18	d	Francis con.	iiij
7	e	Apolina.mar.	v
	f	Faith virgin	vj
15	g	Marce & Mar.	vij
4		Pellagine vir.	viij
	b	Gerdon martir	ix
12	c	Dennis	x
1	d	Nicasius mar.	xj
	e	Wilfride bishop	xij
9	f	Edward king	xiij
	g	[illegible]	xiiij

17		Wolfrane bish.	xv
6	b	Mic. of yͤ moũt	xvj
	c	Etheldred vir.	xvij
14	d	[illegible]	xviij
3	e	Frideswid vir.	xix
	f	Austrebert vir.	xx
11	g	11000. virgins	xxj
19		Mary Salo.	xxij
	b	Romaine bish.	xxiij
8	c	Magior bish.	xxiiij
16	d	Crisp. & Cris.	xxv
	e	Evarist conf.	xxvj
5	f	Fast	xxvij
	g	[illegible]	xxviij
13		Narcis. bish.	xxix
2	b	Germain con.	xxx
	c	Fast	xxxj

Nouẽber hath. xxx. dayes.

The Moone. xxix.

	d	All Saintes.	j
	e	All Soules	ij
18	f	Wenefride vir.	iij
7	g	Amantius	iiij
	A	Lete priest	v
15	b	Leonard conf.	vj
4	c	Wilbrode	vij
	d	Foure crouned	viij
12	e	Theod. mart.	ix
1	f	Martine	x
	g	Martine bish.	xj
9	A	Sun in Sagi.	xij
	b	Paterne mar.	xiij
17	c	Trans. Erken.	xiiij

9	d	Machute bish.	xv
	e	Deposi. Edm.	xvj
14	f	Init. reg. Eliz.	xvij
3	g	Octau. Mar.	xviij
	A	Eliza. matron	xix
11	b	Edmond king	xx
19	c	Presen. of Ma.	xxj
	d	Cicile virgin	xxij
8	e	Clement mar.	xxiij
	f	Grisogon ma.	xxiiij
16	g	Katherin vir.	xxv
5	A	Line martir	xxvj
	b	Ruffin mar.	xxvij
13	c	Nicho. hol.	xxviij
2	d	Fast	xxix
	e	Andrew apo.	xxx

Decēber hath.xxxj. dayes.

The Moone.xxx.

	f	Elegie bishop	j
18	g	Libane martir.	ij
7	A	Depo.of Osm.	iij
	b	Barbara virg.	iiij
15	c	Sabba bishop	v
4	d	Nicholas bishop	vj
	e	Octau.of Andr.	vij
12	f	Concep of Ma.	viij
1	g	Ciprian bishop	ix
	A	Eulalie virgin	x
9	b	[illegible]	xj
	c	Damas.confes.	xij
17	d	Luce virgin	xiij
6	e	Janu.	xiiij

	f	Otholie virgin.	xv
14	g	O sapientia	xvj
3	a	Lazarus bish.	xvij
	b	Gracian bish.	xviij
11	c	Venitia virgin	xix
19	d	Fast.	xx
	e	Thomas apo.	xxj
8	f	xxx. martirs	xxij
	g	Victor virgin	xxiij
16	a	Fast.	xxiiij
5	b	Christmas.	xxv
	c	Steph mar.	xxvj
13	d	John evan.	xxvij
2	e	Innocentes.	xxviij
10	f		xxix
	g	Tran. of Iam.	xxx
	A	Silvester mar.	xxxj

In the name of the father, and of the ſonne and of the holy ghoſt. Amen.

The Lordes prayer.

OUr Father which
art in heauen : ha=
lowed be thy name.
Thy Kyngdome
come. Thy will be done in
earth, as it is in heauē. Giue
vs this day our daylie bread.
And forgiue vs our treſpaſ=
ſes : as wee forgyue them
that treſpaſſe agaynſte vs.
And leade vs not into temp=
tation : but delyuer vs from
euill. Amen.

A

¶ The Beliefe or Creede.

I Beleue in GOD, the father almighthie, maker of heauen and earth: and in Jesus Christe hys onely sonne our Lorde: which was conceiued by the holye Ghoste: borne of the Virgin Mary: suffered vnder Ponce Pilate: was crucifyed, deade and buried: he discended into Hell: the thirde daye hee rose agayne from the deade: he ascended into heauen: and sitteth on the right hande of God the father

father almighty: from thence hee shall come to iudge the quick and the dead. I beleue in the holye ghost: the holye catholike Church: the communion of saintes: the forgiuenesse of sinnes: the resurrection of the bodye: and the lyfe euerlasting. Amen.

The ten Commaundements of almightie God.

Thou shalt haue none other Gods but me.

Thou shalte not make

make to thy selfe anye gra=
uen Image, nor the lyke=
nesse of any thing, that is in
heauen aboue, or in the earth
beneathe, nor in the water
vnder the earth: thou shalt
not bow downe to them, nor
worship them.

iii. Thou shalte not take
the name of the Lorde thy
God in vayne.

iiii. Remember that thou
keepe holy the Saboth day.

v. Honor thy Father, and
thy mother.

vi. Thou shalt do no mur=
ther.

vii. Thou shalt not commit
adulterie.

viii. Thou shalt not steale.

ix. Thou shalt not beare
false wytnesse agaynst thy
neighbour.

x. Thou shalte not desire
thy neighbours house: thou
shalt not couet thy neighbours wyfe, nor hys ser-
uant, nor his Mayde, nor
his Oxe, nor his Asse,
nor any thing that
is thy neigh-
bours.